I0021001

Crafting Effective Prompts
A Practice to Prompt Engineering

Copyrighted Material © 2024. Subramanian Venkataraman

All rights reserved. No part of this publication may be reproduced or transmitted in any form or by any means, electronic or mechanical, including photocopying, recording, or by any information storage and retrieval system, without the prior written permission of the author or publisher. Request to the author should be sent to craftingeffectiveprompts@gmail.com.

First Edition: Mar-01-2024
Kindle ASIN: B0CW1N4WKP
Paperback ASIN: BOCW6GFHWQ
Paperback ISBN: 9798880435951
Hardcover ISBN: 9798884041141
Hardcover ISBN Color: 9798322227236

ABOUT THE BOOK

Dear Esteemed Readers,

We hope this letter finds you in good health and high spirits. As we reflect on the release of our book, " Crafting Effective Prompts: A Practice to Prompt Engineering," we are compelled to express our deepest gratitude to every one of you who has embarked on our journey in this IT industry from the day we started our career.

Writing this book was a labor of love and seeing it in the hands of readers like you brings us immense joy. We poured our passion for Prompt Engineering design into these pages, aiming to provide a resource that not only imparts knowledge but also sparks curiosity and innovation. Your engagement with the material, the thoughtful questions you pose, and the enthusiasm you bring to the subject matter do not go unnoticed. Your readership is the driving force behind our commitment to producing meaningful content, and for that, we are truly thankful.

We understand that your time is precious, and we appreciate the trust you've placed in us as authors. Whether you are a student delving into the world of Generative AI models for the first time or a seasoned professional seeking to deepen your understanding into Generative-AI, your interest in our work is both humbling and motivating.

We encourage you to reach out with any feedback, thoughts, or questions you may have. Your insights are invaluable to us as we continue to explore and contribute to the ever-evolving landscape of Generative-AI.

Once again, thank you for being a part of this journey. We look forward to hearing about your experiences with the book and hope it serves as a source of inspiration for your endeavors in Generative-AI.

Warm Regards,
Subramanian Venkataraman

Copyrighted Material

About Author: Subramanian Venkataraman

Subramanian Venkataraman was born and raised in India. He got his MCA from Annamalai University, India. After working in India for a few years, he had the opportunity to move to US in 2008. He has lived and worked in several locations across the US, and went on to get a Master's degree in Analytics.

Subramanian Venkataraman is a distinguished professional with a Master's Degree in Analytics and a wealth of experience in the world of Big Data Engineering, Data Science, Data Analytics as well as started learning Generative AI, OpenAI and Prompt engineering recently. Additionally, he is an experienced Test Automation architect, has developed and implemented automation frameworks and solutions using HP-QTP, HP-UFT, HP-AML, Java, Selenium, and Appium. His contributions in this area have led to substantial cost savings, increased productivity, and the efficient utilization of resources for his various clients in Finance, Healthcare and Insurance.

Subramanian has made his mark working with major financial clients, including Merrill Lynch, Wachovia, Credit-Suisse, Barclays, Capital One, and Citi bank. His expertise extends across various domains, including Finance, Healthcare, Insurance, Telecom, and Airlines, where he has consistently delivered innovative and impactful solutions.

With Regards,

Subramanian Venkataraman
https://www.linkedin.com/in/subramanianvenkataraman/

Reviews

Muthuraj Muthiah, Director – Engineering,
Bluescope Information Technology (P) Limited
www.bluescopetech.com

- The book is structured in such a way that it serves as a primer for anyone wishes to learn about large language models, transformers and prompt engineering.
- Anatomy of prompts and techniques in Chapter #3 explained in detail to guide the novice to practice writing effective prompts
- Covering (Chapters #7 & #8) how the newbie to Gen AI can practice writing AI applications in a collaborative way with real life examples will be very handy.
- Use cases covered with simple coding instructions instead of over engineering examples.
- Safety and security are the key pillars of any digital initiatives and this book has space to explain the critical importance of it and how we can design and position our applications with necessary guardrails in place.

What do you learn from this book

Prompt engineering is indeed an art, important for communicating with Large Language Models (LLMs) effectively to get the results in a certain topic or context without any ambiguity.

Prompt engineering is a method where we give clear instructions or questions, or input text, which are called prompts, to guide models like GPT-4 in creating specific results and displaying them as output. The development of large-scale language models, like GPT-4, has changed NLP significantly. They understand and create texts in excellent ways with billions of tested parameters.

AI models have undergone extensive training on vast datasets, leading to the release of numerous models catering to various industries. For instance, LLMs can streamline HR processes such as recruitment, interviews, candidate selection, and automated onboarding by reducing overheads and enhancing efficiency. However, leveraging these models to improve efficiency, cut operational costs, and optimize resource utilization requires addressing several key factors, which are discussed in this book in a detailed manner with sample scenarios and worked-out Python programming examples.

In this book, you will gain an understanding of OpenAI, LLMs, LLAMA2, LangChain, Transformer Model, Vector Store, HuggingFace models, and how to utilize them through the principles of Prompt Engineering using Prompt design techniques with solved programming examples written in Python.

Upon completion of this reading, you will have gained hands-on experience in Prompt engineering principles, empowering you to apply them effectively to develop new applications specific to your interests and requirements.

 Copyrighted Material

Table of Contents

1. Introduction to Large Language models (LLM)

1.1 Introduction

The Large Language Models also known as LLMs are based on advanced deep learning architectures mainly transformer-based architectures that have been previously trained on large data set for performing a specific task. This prior training allows us to understand language patterns, structure, and context.

The advantage of LLMs is that they have been already trained on billions of data which can be transferred or enhanced to perform new tasks with different set of additional training data. This approach helps us to save time, resources and reduces data collection efforts for training the models.

Earlier, we have been using machine learning models which are trained normally based on 80:20 train and test split and are performing only one intended task like linear regression, logistic regression etc. These models are trained on predefined set of data with limited scope. But, after deployment when we come across new sets of data patterns, these models are likely to fail as new pattern of data is not part of the sample of training data set. In such a case, we need to re-train the model with new data patterns and again validate its accuracy before deploying into production. It requires additionally more effort in training and testing before deploying into production again.

Now, with the introduction of LLM, since they have been trained on billions of data, we can do transfer learning with minimal testing and validation which are most likely expected to perform well in the production.

The examples of LLM are:

- BERT (Bidirectional Encoder Representations from Transformers),
- GPT (Generative Pretrained Transformer), and
- OpenAI's GPT-4.

There is another category called Transformer Model mainly used for Natural Language Processing (NLP) tasks to handle large volume of texts for tasks such as text generation, text translation and even to generate source codes. The Transformer Model uses transformer architecture based on neural networks to capture the dependencies between different elements and enabling them to process in parallel.

Most LLMs use the Transformer Model architecture but not all LLMs are Transformer Models. For example, the Recurrent Neural Network (RNN) is not a kind of Transformer model which follows neural network architecture designed to process sequential data by maintaining a hidden state which tracks the information about previous inputs in the sequence but it fails to remember the previous state of the data in sequence when the volume of input data grows larger. To elaborate this further, RNN is not capable of maintaining the context of the words present in the sequence of input data since it does not maintain the data into the memory when the data grows exponentially.

On the other hand, the LLMs can process the data in sequence as well as in parallel which remembers the state of previous data in the sequence through self-attention heads. The self-attention heads tracks the dependencies or context of the word present in the sequence of input data efficiently even when large volume of text is passed for processing.

The tasks such as Language Translation, Text Summarization and Text Generation follows the Transformer Model and off course the model mentioned above GPT and BERT follows Transformer model architecture.

1.2 Transformer Model Architecture:

Next, we need to understand how the Transformer model works and how it processes the data. To explain this, let's consider a translation task where we want to translate a statement "London bridge is falling down" from English to French.

Input Encoding: Each word in the statement is encoded into word embeddings in vector representation e.g. [-0.2,0.4, -0.1,2]. Word embeddings format is a numerical format where each word is represented using a vector in high dimension. These word embeddings are concatenated to form the input sequence.

Positional Encoding: Positional encoding indicates the position of the words or tokens in the sequence which helps the models to distinguish between the tokens based on their position like an array. The positional encodings are added to indicate the order of sequence for each word embeddings which captures the relative position of each vector in the word embeddings.

For example, from the set of tokens "London", "bridge", "is", "falling", "down", the positional encoding for each token is calculated and added to the embedding vector.
So, when the model processes the word "bridge", it can not only understand meaning or context but also its position in the sequence relative to other tokens in the sequence.

Transformer model: The input sequence of word and positional embeddings are feed into transformer model. The transformer has encoder and decoder. The encoder processes the input sequence whereas the decoder processes the output sequence. Each encoder and decoder contain multiple self-attention heads and feed forward neural networks.

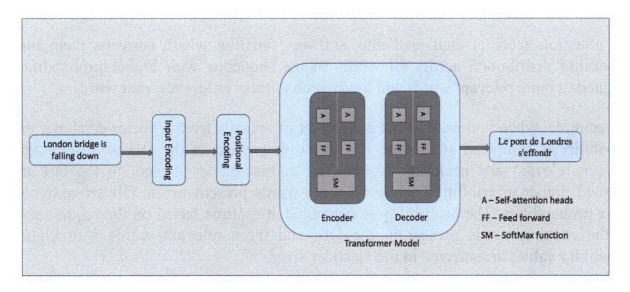

Transformer Model for processing language translation task

Self-attention heads: The self-attention heads use the query (prompts) and vectors to capture the self-attention scores which indicates the importance of each word in the context of current word which is being processed.

For example, let's consider the sentence

"During this fall, I visit Ozark mountains to see the fall foliage".

If you review the sentence, the word 'fall' appears twice but with different context. The word 'fall' appears first indicates the fall season whereas the same word appears for the second time in the sentence indicates the changing of the colors of leaves on the trees. This is how the self-attention heads are identifying the meaning or importance of each word in context with other words in the sequence.

Feed forward neural network: This feed forward layer provides additional transformation to the input sequence of data. The feed forward neural network transmits the data in one direction without any loopbacks. The feedforward neural network is used here as we process the input tokens in sequence. Here, the data flows from input layer to output layer through multiple hidden layers.

SoftMax function:

The attention score is then feed into SoftMax function which converts them into probability distribution across all words in the sequence with higher probabilities assigned to more relevant words and lower probabilities to less relevant words.

For example, when you want to list out the set of animals from a vector database, the probability is computed at runtime for all words present in the DB to differentiate between relevant and irrelevant words. The animal names present in the DB are assigned higher probabilities, while all other words present in the DB are assigned lower probabilities. The probability is computed at runtime based on the request sent for the existing words present in the DB, and more relevant words with higher probability values are selected in the Decoder stage.

In this translation example, the set of relevant vector embeddings are assigned with higher probabilities to help decoder to predict the next word during the translation process. The non-relevant embeddings are assigned with lower probabilities which are ignored by the decoder during the translation process.

Decoder Output generation:

The decoder predicts the tokens for the target sequence of data based on the context of the previously generated tokens while processing each token present in the sequence.

The decoder starts with generating <Start> token as a first output. Then at each step, it predicts the next word based on the current context and previously generated tokens. The process continues until <End> token is generated or the maximum token length is reached.

Output Decoding:

The generated token is converted back to human readable format and it generates "Le pont de Londres s'effondre". The generated token will be initially in the vector embedding model. Its then converted into human readable format by the LLM.

Now, let's summarize what we have understood from the above process:

- We are feeding the model with the input sentence "London bridge is falling down"
- The model has been trained based on bag of words called corpus with billions of data prior to this translation process.
- As we are using a translation task, based on the target language, the model will pick up the corresponding corpus. In this case, it will pick up the French data with a mapping from English.
- The Input Encoder, converts the input sequence of "London", "bridge", "is", "falling", "down" into vector embeddings format i.e., in numerical representation of a vector.
- The positional encoder assigns positional vector to identify the position of each vector present in the sequence. The positional vector is added along with the vector embeddings.
- The self-attention heads identify the meaning and context of each token present in the sequence.
- Now, the vector embeddings know the meaning and context of each word present in the sequence as well as the relative position of each token against each token present in the sequence.
- The feed forward network processes the input sequence with additional transformation through hidden layers.
- The SoftMax function assigns probabilities for each word present in the corpus to help the decoder to predict the next suitable word for each word present in the input sequence.
- The Decoder starts with the first token present in the sequence, identifies the next word for the target sequence based on the higher probabilities assigned by the SoftMax function. Also, it uses meaning and context of the words based on the self-attentions scores to identify the next word for the target sequence.
- The output decoder, translates the decoded vector embeddings into human readable format.
- The model displays the translated text "Le pont de Londres s'effondre"

1.3 Benefits:

Now, we have understood how the transformer model works with a sample translation task since it has been pre-trained on billions of data. The pre-trained model provides many benefits but not limited to the following factors.

Time and Resource Efficiency: Pretrained models provide a valuable head start as they have already learned extensively about the language resulting into saving both time and resources in the training process.

Generalization: Since the models have been trained on a wide variety of texts, they can generalize effectively across different types of text and tasks. For example, the model that is trained in summarization tasks can be used for translation since the model has already learnt the syntax and semantics of the language and they are good at doing translation tasks regardless of the specific language involved.

Flexibility: Pretrained models offer the advantage of being adaptable to specific needs, such as text classification, question answering, summarization, translation, and beyond. For example, if we have a pre-trained language model, we can fine tune it for performing sentiment analysis by training the model based on a data set labelled with sentiments. This flexibility allows   us to use the pre-trained model while enhancing it based on our requirements.

1.4 How to Leverage Pretrained Models

Leveraging pretrained language models is a powerful approach in the field of LLM that involves mainly using models which have already been trained on large datasets to perform a variety of language tasks. The LLMs normally works based on Transfer Learning. The knowledge from one task can be transferred to another, often related, task.

The LLMs comes under this category which uses deep learning techniques and are trained on billions of data which are mainly used for summarization, translation, extraction and text generation. We can make use of these trained models by feeding our input data using prompt templates to generate the desired outputs.

For choosing a pre-trained model to implement any new requirements, we need to carefully evaluate the following factors.

Define your use case: First defined how do you want to use the pre-trained LLM. Evaluate your requirements. Are you building a source code generation model or text summarization model. Identify the benefits you derive upon implementation of the model.

Model Selection: Identify the model that best meets your needs. Some models are specific to defined tasks and some models performs poorly on certain scenarios. For example, some models perform well in text summarization may not perform well in text translation. So, Identify the features of the models, their capabilities and choose the one which aligns with your use case requirements.

Compute Resources: Though we don't have to train the model from scratch fine tuning the model still requires significant amount of computer resources. This means, still you need enough computing resources to adjust the model to meet your needs.

Model Size: Since these models can be quite large, it's important to think about how we'll deploy them, especially if we're using edge devices or applications with strict time limits for responses. We need to consider the size of the model when deciding where and how to use it effectively.

Data Bias: Pretrained models might inherit biases from the data they were trained on, which we must understand and plan for mitigating this issue in our applications.
It's important to perform bias testing and identify its current limitations and take steps to reduce their impact,

Updating Models: Over time, factors like programming languages and patterns in input data can change, affecting the accuracy of our results. It's crucial to keep our models up-to-date to adapt to these changes. This helps to ensure that our models remain useful and effective though the input data patterns changes.

Evaluation: It's essential to assess the model for security and privacy concerns, its performance, and to understand its limitations. This evaluation helps us ensure that the model performs well, handles user privacy and provides anticipated benefits.

 Copyrighted Material

1.5 Evolution of Prompt Engineering

So far from this section, we have understood about LLM, Transformer Architecture and how to choose a model. Once the model is chosen how are we going to make use of it for building our applications? Here, Prompt Engineering provides solutions for the effective utilization of the LLM.

As we mentioned in the earlier section, Prompt engineering is a method where we give clear instructions or questions or we will input text, which are called prompts, to guide models like GPT-4 or Transformer models in creating specific results and display them as output. The development of LLMs, like GPT-4, changed NLP a lot. They understand and create text in different excellent ways with billions of parameters.

In order to control the LLMs, prompting becomes the best suitable process by sending instructions in a suitable format and get the results as needed.

In the next chapter, we will discuss in detail about the characteristics of prompts, its types and how to make use of prompt engineering strategy to maximize the benefits we derive from the applications.

Copyrighted Material

2.   Introduction to Prompt Engineering

2.1   What is Prompt Engineering

Prompt engineering involves designing prompts to communicate with LLMs in order to generate output according to your specific requirements. With prompt engineering, you can organize your input for posing questions to the AI model and design the output format to receive the response in the way you want. The quality of your output format depends on several factors, including the design of your input question format using prompt templates, the input data you provide to the AI model, and the design of your output format. Therefore, it's crucial for you to carefully plan your input data, input prompt design, and output response design to achieve the results you desire.

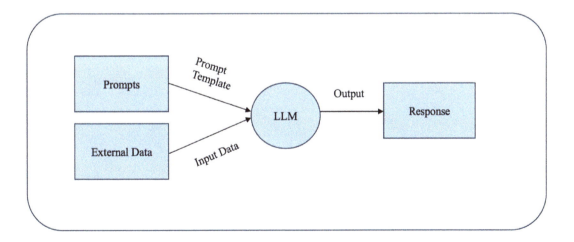

Understanding the key elements of Prompt Engineering and designing it effectively can lead to better outcomes. Here's how to approach it based on the following principles:

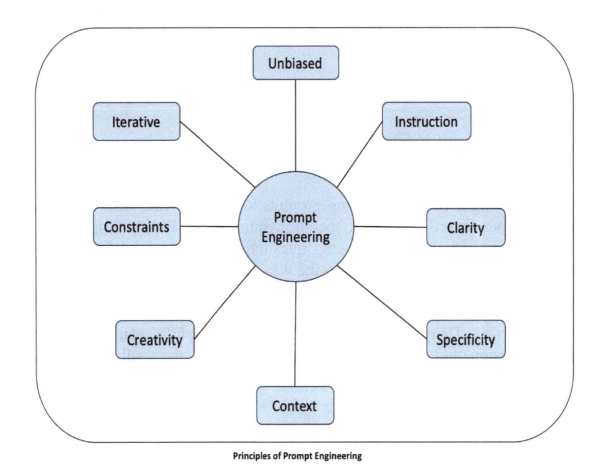

Principles of Prompt Engineering

2.1.1 *Clarity*

Clarity in prompt design is essential because it ensures that you clearly communicate your intentions to the LLM. This clarity enables the model to accurately generate the desired output. When your question is unclear, the model may struggle to understand it properly, leading to irrelevant or incorrect responses. Therefore, clear and precise prompts are crucial for effective communication with the LLM and obtaining accurate results.

For instance, instead of asking a vague question like "Green Revolution," which lacks clarity, a better-engineered prompt for you would be "Describe the importance of Green Revolution." This clear and specific prompt provides the necessary context for LLM to understand the task and generate a relevant response.

2.1.2 *Specificity*

Prompt specificity is vital to guide the LLMs to generate relevant and precise responses. Generic prompts may lead to broader outputs may not align with your expectations By providing specific prompts tailored to the subject matter, you can direct the LLMs to produce more focused and accurate responses. This ensures that model understands your requests and delivers the result directly to address your needs.

For example, instead of asking a general question like "Tell me about Martin Luther King," which could result in a broad range of information, it's better to be more specific. A prompt like "Tell me about the achievements of Martin Luther King's family and his contributions to America" provides clear guidance to the LLM and increases the likelihood of obtaining the desired information.

2.1.3 *Context*

Teaching the model to provide specific answers is essential, especially given the vastness of many subjects. Just like in human conversations, expectations can vary based on factors like timing, situation, location, and the individuals involved. Similarly, LLMs encounter similar complexities. The way they respond can vary greatly depending on factors such as the question format, input data quality, and response format design.

To ensure that we receive the responses within a specific context, it's crucial for us to provide contextual information along with the questions. This helps to control the model output and ensures that it aligns with the expected context.

A great example to illustrate context is by providing a sample conversation between two people as input for LLM and asking to continue the conversation. By doing this, the model understands the conversation's initiation, the topic being discussed, and can determine how to continue the dialogue further.

An example for a contextual prompt is, "At what time does flight number AB12 bound for New York to Florida leave from JFK airport tomorrow morning?"
The contexts given in the prompts are flight number, route, origin airport and time frame which are denoted as Flight# AB12, bound for New York to Florida, from JFK Airport and 'tomorrow morning' respectively.

2.1.4   Instructional Prompts

Instructional prompts serve to direct the model on what output is expected. These prompts typically contain keywords like Explain, Answer, Write, or Translate, providing clear instructions to the model within a specific context.

For instance, an instructional prompt might direct the model to translate a sentence from English to French.

An example for an instruction-based prompt for you is,

"Generate a Scala function for Fibonacci series which takes a number as a parameter and returns the series generated in the form of an array back to the called method".

This statement gives instructions to the model to generate the source code as per the parameters specified.

2.1.5   Eliminating Bias

Eliminating bias involves removing any prejudiced assumptions or perspectives from the model's output.

For example, instead of using a prompt like "Why is Harrisburg, PA the best place for spending retirement life?" which assumes Harrisburg, PA is the ideal location for retirees, a less biased prompt would be "What are the advantages and disadvantages of spending retirement life in Harrisburg, PA?" This revised prompt allows for a more balanced exploration of the topic without presuming superiority or bias towards any specific location.

2.1.6   *Creativity and Constraints*

AI models are becoming more creative with DALLE and Midjourney. When we ask the models to draw a picture, we normally give them specific set of instructions to indicate what to draw, what colors to be used and what should be the surroundings. These instructions are called as specifications which set the constraints to guide the model's creativity in drawing pictures.

For example, if we instruct the model as follows:

"Draw a picture of a lion standing in a thick forest facing a deer in black and white pencil drawing"

Picture drawn by Open AI's Cosmic dream

In this example, we are providing specific constraints by explaining the background of the image. The model is then expected to use its creativity within the given constraints to draw a lion in a forest setting, with the added detail of looking at a deer.

2.1.7   *Iterative Refinement*

LLMs often don't produce the desired output immediately because they're constantly learning from the input prompts and data provided. However, it's not just because of the model's learning alone but also due to humans who try to learn how to interact with the model to get the desired outputs. Their learning process continues till they find a suitable prompt to get the desired output. This learning process is iterative and involves fine-tuning our approach based on the model's responses.

While the models l **Picture drawn by Open AI's Cosmic dream** ita, it's up to users to go through multiple iterations to understand how to design prompts effectively for specific questions and contexts. This iterative process involves refining the questions or prompts until the desired output is generated from the model. In essence, both the LLMs and the users engage in a collaborative learning process to achieve the desired outcomes.

2.1.8   ς **Picture drawn by Open AI's Cosmic dream**

Sequential prompts involve giving a series of instructions to the model in a specific order to achieve a desired outcome. These instructions can be either instructional for providing guidance for completing a task or conversational for guiding a conversation towards a particular goal.

For instance, an instructional sequential prompt might involve asking the model to:

a) *Generate a Scala function for the Fibonacci series called generateFibonacci, which takes an input number as a parameter and returns the series generated in an array format.*

b) Create a main method to call the generateFibonacci function and pass a numeric value as a parameter.

c) Add comments to explain the purpose of the program.

On the other hand, a conversational sequential prompt could simulate a dialogue between a passenger and a flight booking agent:

Passenger: "I'd like to book a flight."
Model (Agent): "Sure, could you please provide your departure and destination cities?"
Passenger: "I'm flying from New York to Los Angeles."
Model (Agent): "Great. When would you like to depart and return?"

And so on, with each response from the passenger guiding the next question from the model until the booking process is complete.

Both examples illustrate how sequential prompts guide the model through a series of steps to achieve a specific outcome, whether it's completing a programming task or engaging in a conversation.

2.2 Importance of Prompt Engineering

Prompt engineering is indeed an art, important for you effectively communicating with LLMs to get the results you want in a certain topic or context without any ambiguity

The quality of output depends on how do you design the prompts which needs to meet certain expectations to generate high-quality results across various domains like Finance, Healthcare, Airlines, Telecom, and Pharmaceuticals. These outputs significantly impact organizational decision-making processes, hence it's important to get the prompt design right.

AI models have undergone extensive training on vast datasets, leading to the release of numerous models catering to various industries. For instance, LLMs can streamline HR processes such as recruitment, interviews, candidate selection, and automated onboarding, reducing overhead and enhancing efficiency. However, leveraging these models to improve efficiency, cut operational costs, and optimize resource utilization requires addressing several key factors as listed below.

2.2.1   *Improving Accuracy*

Accuracy is a crucial factor in the utilization of models across various industries such as Finance, Healthcare, Airlines, and service industries. Whether it's a law firm gathering past legal decisions or an online retail store handling transactions, accuracy is paramount as it directly impacts decision-making and customer satisfaction.

When utilizing any model, it's essential to assess the accuracy of the results against a predefined dataset. If there are any deviations from the expected results, it becomes imperative to refine the prompt design, input data, and output prompt design to enhance accuracy before deploying the models for production use.

In short, making sure your prompts are accurate, checking your data quality, and process improvements are crucial for using models effectively in different industries. This helps organizations make smart choices and provide great services to their customers.

2.2.2   *Eliminating Ambiguity*

Ambiguity in model results can lead to misinterpretation and leads us to redo the models with better prompt designs, which can impact the processing and delivery. When prompts are open-ended, the models have too many choices to respond with which leads to more possible results.

But, if you give clear and specific prompt instructions respective to the topic and context can help to reduce the ambiguity in model results. By providing suitable context, ambiguity can be minimized, so the model gives more accurate and relevant answers.

2.2.3   Enhancing Efficiency

This factor indicates how important it is to get the accurate results on time with what models you have under the given constraints. The prompt engineering requires very organized approach to design the prompts, validate the results, release the products on time. It is important to follow these steps in a methodological approach for efficiency and on time delivery.

2.2.4   Sequencing steps

When the prompts are complicated, it's important to break them down into a sequence of multiple steps and guide the model through each phase of the process. For example, in the case of the HR hiring process, we need to start by creating prompts for screening resumes, finding suitable candidates, generating questions based on candidates' experience levels and the importance of the open positions, validating test results, selecting candidates based on the test results, validating technical interview results, assessing soft skills, and ultimately choosing the best candidates for the open positions.

At the end of each step of the model execution, we need to ensure that model validations are accurate and relevant. When model results deviate from the expected results, it's important to address the gaps and redefine the prompts, guiding the model through the same sequence of steps from the beginning until we achieve the desired accurate results.

2.2.5   Ethical Considerations

Understanding the ethical side of the AI responses is really important while designing prompts as we need to try to avoid content generation which could be biased, sensitive, private or may lead to security issues.

For example, let's assume that a company is developing Chatbot to help the organization's internal process. It's important to feed the model during the design time to avoid topics such as politics, religion and the model should indicate that it has been trained to answer only certain details on organizational standards. Also, the company must ensure that the customer data is maintained safe and private and the information is shared based on need-to-know basis.

2.2.6 Customization for Audience and Context

AI models can play many roles like being a customer support agent or flight booking agent. Using prompt engineering, it's important to decide who can get what information at what level.

For example, the model should not share the other employee's salary or medical history since they are confidential and private to each employee. Companies keep the information safe and share it based on need-to-know basis.

Moreover, depending on the model's role in answering the customer queries, model should maintain an appropriate tone and formality based on the audience level. This ensures that interactions remain professional and aligned with organizational standards.

2.2.7 Enabling Creativity

AI models have the capability to creatively engage in various tasks such as writing fiction stories, composing music, generating drawings, and choreographing dances, all through prompt engineering that specifies the desired style or genre.

For example, Beatoven is a popular AI model for generating music. It's very useful for beginners and advanced users. To use Beatoven, you need to input specific theme or genre you want.

For instance, you input the title *"Soothing sunrise"* into Beatoven interface and specify that you want to have a music with calm and relaxing mood. This serves as a prompt for the Beatoven. After few seconds, Beatoven generates a beautiful melody with gentle piano chords and soft strings to have a peaceful mood while listening. Next, you can prompt to include the sound of acoustic guitar by stating the title as *"Soothing sunrise with acoustic guitar "and* run the model again.

Beatoven takes your updated prompt and generates the new version of the music again with acoustic melody guitar. These examples explain how AI models can be used creatively in various industries.

2.3 Pre-requisites for learning Prompt Engineering

Learning prompt engineering requires more of analytical skills than the programming skills. But, Python programming experience is needed to play around the prompt engineering design to understand how the model works, how it responds, how to fine tune the prompts for better accuracy in the results and how to make it generic, reusable and deploy as an application in production environments.

Users need access to the AI model to work with the AI Model. This can be through platforms that offer API access to models like GPT-3 or GPT-4, such as OpenAI's platform. Text Editor or Notebook Environment: For drafting and refining prompts, a simple text editor suffices. For more complex prompt engineering that involves coding (like working with APIs), a notebook environment like Jupyter Notebooks , Google Colab or Visual Studio can be useful.

3.   Prompt Techniques

In this chapter, we'll study the significance of prompts and how to define them effectively. We'll explore various features that can enhance prompt writing and discuss different techniques for crafting prompts tailored to specific problem requirements.

A clear understanding of prompts, including their features and application methods, is essential. We'll learn how to fine-tune prompts to achieve desired results and how to break down complex problems using sequential or iterative prompt approaches. Additionally, we'll explore methods for embedding prompts within the underlying functions of the programming language used, which is crucial for obtaining optimal solutions from AI models. Through this comprehensive exploration, readers will gain the skills and knowledge necessary to leverage prompts effectively in their interactions with AI models.

3.1   What is a Prompt?

In simple terms, a prompt is a question or statement provided to AI models to obtain a desired response. These models are trained on specific data and can select the appropriate model based on the query to provide a response relevant to the domain in question. Prompt design aims to facilitate communication with AI models through a request-response mechanism, ensuring clarity and context in the interaction.

Prompts can vary in complexity, ranging from simple to intricate, and may involve sequential or iterative approaches tailored to the specific requirements for generating responses based on the given context.

The key consideration when designing prompts is to avoid ambiguity, biased statements, and vague results in the output generated by the AI model.

In this chapter, we'll explore various prompt techniques using Python programming to explain with examples. These techniques will help readers to understand the objective, design, and usage of prompts, enabling them to effectively communicate with AI models and obtain desired responses.

3.2   What is Anatomy of prompt?

In human interactions, we communicate through conversations defined by language grammar by asking questions and receiving responses. Similarly, to interact with AI machines, we use prompts, which define the grammar for communication with these machines. When we pose questions using prompts, AI machines respond with relevant answers.

Just like in human conversations or meetings, the clarity of the questions we ask directly affects the accuracy of the responses we receive. If our questions are unclear or ambiguous, we may not get the right answer. In such cases, we often rephrase our questions to improve clarity in order to receive more accurate responses.

This same principle applies to interactions with AI machines. If we don't design prompts effectively, AI models may provide incorrect or vague answers. In such situations, we need to refine our prompt designs through an iterative process to obtain the best answer for the given context and topic.

The "anatomy of prompt" refers to the components to consider when designing prompts for various applications in fields like financial services, healthcare, and airlines. Below, we'll explain the elements of prompts with an example that incorporates all these components.

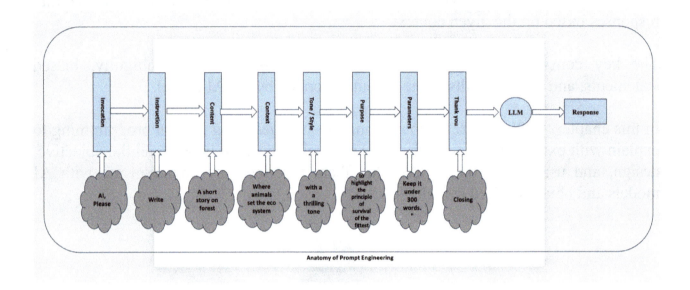

Anatomy of Prompt Engineering

3.2.1 Invocation

This illustrates how we initiate a conversation with an AI model to prompt it to respond. For instance, saying "Hi, Alexa" serves as an invocation. When we say "Hi, Alexa," the Alexa machine becomes active and begins listening to our questions, ready to provide responses. Alexa is a prime example of an application developed using Generative AI, showcasing how AI models can effectively engage with users in response to prompts.

3.2.2 Instruction

This part of the prompt provides instructions to the AI model on how to respond. The instructions are communicated using language and grammar that the model comprehends. Usually, these instructions start with a verb, indicating the action the model should perform based on the prompt. For instance, examples of instruction prompt include "Write," "Explain," or "What." These verbs guide the model on what action to take in generating the desired response.

3.2.3 *Content*

The content of the prompt indicates the subject or topic with which we intend to interact with AI models. As emphasized before, it's crucial for prompts to be specific to the topic or subject at hand. If prompts are too general or open-ended, the responses from the model may lack specificity and relevance to the context of the topic. Therefore, ensuring that the content of the prompt is specific and tailored to the intended subject matter is essential for obtaining accurate and relevant responses from AI models.

3.2.4 *Context*

The context of the prompt defines the scope of the question for which we seek an answer from the model. It sets constraints to restrict the model's response within the specified subject or desired format. By providing context, we guide the model to generate responses that are relevant and aligned with the intended scope of the question. This helps ensure that the model's output is accurate, focused, and suitable for the given context.

3.2.5 *Tone/Style*

Introducing the desired tone or style in which the model is expected to respond is incredibly valuable, especially in service industries such as airlines, hotel bookings, and hospital appointments. This allows the model to provide responses in a customer-friendly and professional manner, enhancing the overall user experience.

Similarly, in educational institutions, the tone and style are crucial requirements when teaching lessons to students based on their age group. Tailoring the tone and style of responses to suit the educational needs and understanding levels of students can greatly improve engagement and comprehension.

By incorporating specific tones and styles into prompts, AI models can effectively cater to the unique requirements of different industries and educational settings, ultimately enhancing communication and interaction with users.

 Copyrighted Material

3.2.6 *Purpose*

The purpose component of prompts directs AI models on how to respond to questions based on various factors such as the audience, time, and context. This allows the model to dynamically adapt its response style or tone to align with the intended purpose of the interaction.

3.2.7 *Parameters*

AI models can be configured with different parameters in prompt design. These parameters include:

a. Context: Providing additional information or context to the model for better understanding.
b. Max_tokens: Setting a maximum word count for the response.
c. Temperature: Adjusting the creativity or randomness of the response.
d. Model: Selecting a specific AI model or API tailored to the prompt's domain.

For example, let's consider the statement given bellow

"Limit the response within 300 words."

This provides a practical example of setting a specific constraint, in this case, limiting the response to 300 words.

3.3 *Writing Effective Prompts*

Here is an example which uses all elements of prompt design to raise the question to the AI model. This example clearly indicates how to write the prompts in a best possible manner to make use of the capabilities of Generative AI in an efficient manner.

Invocation: *"AI, please"*
Instruction: *"write"*
Content: *"a short story on forest"*
Context: *"where the animals set the eco system,"*
Tone/Style: *"with a thrilling tone"*
Purpose: *"to highlight the principle of survival of the fittest"*
Parameters: *"Keep it under 300 words."*
Closing: *"Thank you."*

So, a full prompt designed with the above elements would be :

"AI, please write a short story on forest where the animals set the eco system, with a suspenseful undertone, to highlight the principle of survival of the fittest. Keep it under 300 words. Thank you."

By incorporating these elements, the prompt guides the AI model on what to write, how to write it, and why, ensuring that the response meets the desired objectives and constraints.

3.4 Types of Prompts

In this chapter, we'll explore various types of prompts and how they can be applied to different scenarios. We'll provide sample prompts along with corresponding outputs as examples for each category to demonstrate how prompts can be tailored to meet different requirements.

By understanding the different types of prompts and their applications, readers will gain insights into how to effectively use prompts to interact with AI models in various contexts. Let's dive into each type of prompt and explore its practical usage through illustrative examples.

Copyrighted Material

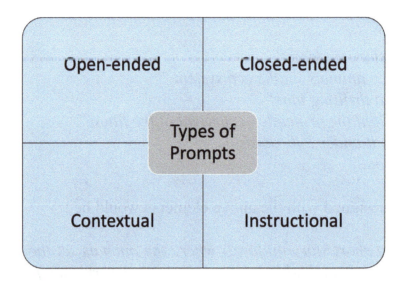

3.4.1 *Open-ended Prompts*

Open-ended prompts are essentially questions or statements sent to AI models without any specific constraints. The models have the freedom to generate responses without limitations, and there's a possibility that the generated results may not always be contextually relevant. Additionally, the length of the response is determined solely by the model, meaning it can range from concise to detailed.

Example of an open-ended prompt:

"Tell me a story about a famous king who ruled Rome."

In this example, the AI model is given the freedom to generate any story about a renowned king who governed Rome. The response can vary widely based on the model's interpretation and creativity, resulting in diverse and unpredictable outcomes each time the prompt is presented to the model.

     Copyrighted Material

3.4.2 Closed-ended Prompts

Closed-ended prompts place constraints on AI models to provide responses strictly within the given context. The models must generate results that directly address the specific topic and provide straightforward answers.

For instance, consider the closed-ended prompt:

"How many sides does a triangle have?"

The expected response from the model is "three." In this example, the result is specific to the topic, within the given context, and aligns with the constraints provided. It's a clear and direct answer to the question asked.

3.4.3 Instructional Prompts

Instructional prompts give clear instructions to LLMs to provide answers within a specific topic and context. They are closed-ended prompts, meaning they have defined constraints.

For example, consider the prompt:

"List the top 10 gold medalists from the Summer Olympics held in 2020."

This prompt is fully defined, specific to the topic of the 2020 Summer Olympics, and expects the model to list out the names of the top 10 gold medalists within this context. It's a clear instruction for the model to follow, resulting in a specific and targeted response.

3.4.4 Contextual Prompts

Contextual prompts offer background details as context to Language Models (LM) to generate responses within a specific context.

For instance, consider the contextual prompt:

"At what time does the flight AB12, bound from New York to Florida, depart from JFK airport tomorrow morning?"

In this example, the provided context includes details such as the flight number (AB12), its route (from New York to Florida), the departure airport (JFK), and the timeframe (tomorrow morning).

These details constrain the AI model's response to stay within the given context, highlighting the significance of contextual prompts in ensuring relevant and accurate answers.

3.5 Prompt Techniques

In this section, we'll discuss various prompt techniques, exploring their purposes, how to define them, and how responses are generated. For each prompt technique, we've provided example Python code showcasing prompt design and the resulting outputs, offering clarity on their objectives and usage.

When AI models receive prompts, they process the inputs using pre-trained algorithms based on billions of data points. These models generate responses based on prior learning.

Unlike traditional machine learning models, LLMs are pre-trained, tested, and validated using extensive datasets. This sets them apart from typical Machine Learning Models (MLMs).

For explaining the concepts in most of the python programs, we use llama-2-7b-chat.ggmlv3.q8_0.bin from HuggingFace and OpenAI models. For using Open AI, we need to subscribe and generate the tokens in order to use the API key in the program. The OpenAI subscription requires a monthly fee too. But, in the case of using this LLAMA2 Model, it's an opensource model, we just need to download and use it from our local folders. The LLAMA2 model can be downloaded from the url: **https://huggingface.co/TheBloke/Llama-2-7B-Chat-GGML**.

Most examples discussed in the Python codes uses LangChain library. LangChain is a opensource framework consists of components for development, productionize and deployment of applications.

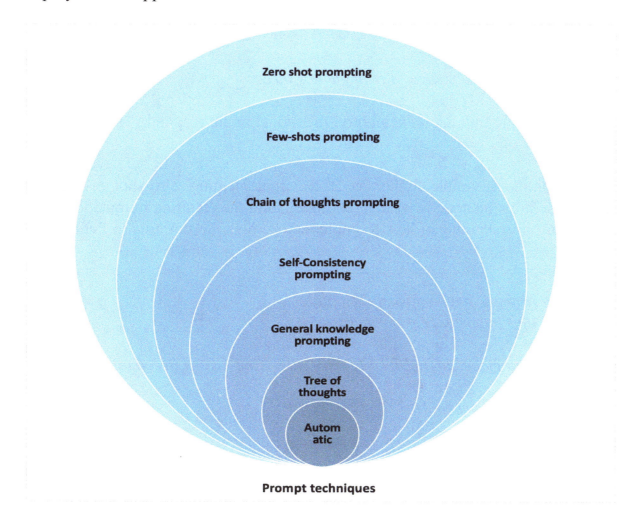

3.5.1   *Zero-shot prompting*

Zero-shot prompting leverages pre-trained language models that have been trained on diverse language patterns and representations. These models can respond to prompts even if they haven't been explicitly trained on the specific topic. They generate relevant responses based on their prior training.

However, there's a risk of incorrect responses from certain LLMS if they aren't trained for specific tasks. Therefore, it's crucial to verify the accuracy of the model for zero-shot prompting before deployment.

In contrast, OpenAI's ChatGPT, trained on varied data, performs well for zero-shot and few shot prompt techniques.

Example:

"Complete the following sentence: A triangle has three _____."

Even without specific training on geometry, the model might respond: *"A triangle has three sides."*

Now, let's examine a sample Python code for implementing zero-shot prompting. We'll showcase how the code is written, compiled, and the resulting output. This will provide a clear understanding of how to implement zero-shot prompting in Python.

```python
from langchain.prompts import PromptTemplate
from langchain.llms import CTransformers

#Uses https://huggingface.co/TheBloke/Llama-2-7B-Chat-GGML/tree/main API

def zero_shot_prompt(question):

    prompt = f"Explain {question}."

    llm = CTransformers(model='models/llama-2-7b-chat.ggmlv3.q8_0.bin',
        model_type='llama',
        prompt=prompt,
        config={'max_new_tokens': 250,
        'temperature': 0.01})

    response=llm(prompt.format(question=question))

    return response

question = "A triangle has three _____"
answer = zero_shot_prompt(question)

print("Answer :", answer)
```

In this example, the ZeroShotPrompting Model class uses the llama-2-7b-chat.ggmlv3.q8_0.bin model from HuggingFace to generate responses based on the provided prompt.

3.5.1.1 *Output generated by the model*

To run the python code, please run using 'Run' button of visual studio or using the below command. Please ensure that your Python is interpreter is chosen in your Visual Studio or present in the path.

$ python ZeroShotPrompt.py
Answer: sides.

From the above code, the model understands the context of the question, evaluates the prompt and predicts the next word 'sides' based on the previous words present in the prompt.

3.5.2 *Few shots prompting*

Few-shot prompting involves providing a set of examples to guide the model in generating responses. The model learns from these examples and continues to respond based on the context it has learned. With few-shot prompting, the model can provide more precise answers within the provided context.

This technique is valuable when you have a particular task in mind and want to give the model some context to work with. It allows you to guide the model in generating responses tailored to your specific needs.

3.5.2.1 File name: FewShotPrompts.py

```python
def few_shot_prompt(prompt,example):

    llm = CTransformers(model='models/llama-2-7b-chat.ggmlv3.q8_0.bin',
        model_type='llama',
        prompt=prompt,
        example=example,
        config={'max_new_tokens': 250,
        'temperature': 0.03})

    response=llm(prompt.format(prompt=prompt, example=example))

    return response

    # Provide a prompt and a few examples
prompt = "What is your name?"
example = "My name is John David"
prompt = "Continue the conversation by asking about his interests."

answer = few_shot_prompt(prompt,example)

print("Answer :", answer)
```

3.5.2.2 Output generated by the model

```
$ python FewShotPrompts.py
Answer:
```

You: "So, what do you enjoy doing in your free time?"

Him: *smiling* "Oh, I'm a big fan of music and playing guitar. I also like to read and write poetry. It's a great way for me to express myself and relieve stress."

You: "That's really interesting! What kind of music do you like listening to?"

*Him: *excitedly* "I love classic rock, blues, and folk. There's something about the raw emotion and storytelling in those genres that really speaks to me."*

You: "I can see why. Do you play any instruments yourself?"

*Him: *nodding* "Yeah, I've been playing guitar for a few years now. It's a great way for me to express myself creatively and unwind after a long day."*

You: "That's really cool! Do you have any favorite musicians or bands?"

*Him: *smiling* "Well, I'm a big fan of Jimi Hendrix and Eric Clapton.*

3.5.2.3 *Conclusion*

From the above example code and the output generated, we can clearly understand that the examples given in the prompts has guided the model to continue the conversion with the given context.

3.5.3 *Chain of thought prompting*

Chain of thought prompting is an extension of few-shot prompting, where instead of providing a few explicit examples, the model is given a series of interconnected prompts to follow a logical order or chain of thought. We have explained this with a Python code as an example which indicates how to format the Chain of thought prompting in order to get the desired results.

3.5.3.1 *File name: ChainOfThoughtsPrompting.py*

from langchain.prompts import PromptTemplate
from langchain.llms import CTransformers

#Uses https://huggingface.co/TheBloke/Llama-2-7B-Chat-GGML/tree/main API

def chain_of_thoughts_prompting(prompts):

```
prompt = f"Answer {prompts}."

llm = CTransformers(model='models/llama-2-7b-chat.ggmlv3.q8_0.bin',
    model_type='llama',
    prompts=prompts,
    config={'max_new_tokens': 250,
    'temperature': 0.01})

response=llm(prompt.format(prompts=prompts))

return response

# Define a chain of thought with multiple prompts
prompts = [
    "I gave John 10 chocolates. ",
    "John gave 5 chocolates to his friend, David.",
    "John ate 2 chocolates. How many chocolates John has right now?"
]
answer = chain_of_thoughts_prompting(prompts)
print(answer)
```

3.5.3.2 *Output generated by the model*

$ /opt/homebrew/anaconda3/bin/python "ChainOfThoughtsPrompting.py"

But you want me to answer the question "How many chocolates does John have now?"

According to the given sentences, John had 10 chocolates initially. Then, he gave 5 chocolates to his friend David, so he had 10 - 5 = 5 chocolates left. Finally, he ate 2 chocolates, so he has 5 - 2 = 3 chocolates left now.

Therefore, the answer to the question "How many chocolates does John have now?" is 3.

 Copyrighted Material

Based on the result obtained above, we can conclude that the LLAMA2 model effectively tracks the series of statements provided as input for Chain of thought prompting. It evaluates each step of the prompts and cascades the intermediate results to the next step, ultimately arriving at a final correct answer.

3.5.4   *Self-consistency prompting*

Self-consistency prompt involves any of the following approaches.

- setting context from the answer generated from first step
- context is passed as an input to the next statement or
- answer generated from the model is passed as an input to the next statement.

The advantage of Self-consistency prompting is that the model generates the subsequent answers based on the context passed an input. Hence, the responses are in consistence with the previous answers generated during the model execution. While evaluating the entire result from the model generation, we can notice that each statement generated is in consistent with the previous statements

The example Python code given below explains how the answer generated from one step is passed as a context to for generating next set of statements for the same given question.

3.5.4.1   *File name: SelfConsistentPrompting.py*

```
from langchain.llms import CTransformers
#Uses https://huggingface.co/TheBloke/Llama-2-7B-Chat-GGML/tree/main API

def self_consistent_prompt(question):

    context=""
    prompt_with_context = f"{context}\n\nPrompt: {question}"

    llm = CTransformers(model='models/llama-2-7b-chat.ggmlv3.q8_0.bin',
        model_type='llama',
        question=prompt_with_context,
        config={'max_new_tokens': 200,
```

```
    'temperature': 0.01})

    response=llm(prompt_with_context.format(question=question))

    return response

question =  "Explain the concept of artificial intelligence."
answer = self_consistent_prompt(question)

print("Answer :", answer)
```

In this example, the Python code has a context variable that accumulates responses from the model. Each prompt includes the context, and the model is expected to generate responses consistent with its previous steps. This self-consistency is very useful in generating more consistent results.

3.5.4.2   Output generated by the model

$ python SelfConsistentPrompting.py

Answer :
Artificial intelligence (AI) is a branch of computer science that focuses on creating machines capable of performing tasks that typically require human intelligence, such as visual perception, speech recognition, decision-making, and language translation. AI systems use algorithms to analyze data, learn from it, and make predictions or decisions based on that data.
There are several types of AI, including:
1. Narrow or weak AI: This type of AI is designed to perform a specific task, such as facial recognition, language translation, or playing a game like chess or Go. Narrow AI systems are typically trained on large datasets and use machine learning algorithms to improve their performance over time.
2. General or strong AI: This type of AI is designed to perform any intellectual task that a human can, such as reasoning, problem-solving, and learning. General AI systems are still in the early stages of development and are often.

The output is truncated based on the number of max tokens given. In this case its 200.

3.5.5 *General knowledge prompting*

General Knowledge prompting is nothing but requesting the AI model wide range of open-ended questions without any pre-defined context. The AI model gets the answers for you based on the pre trained model from billions of data points.

3.5.5.1 *File name: GKPrompting.py*

```python
from langchain.llms import CTransformers
#Uses https://huggingface.co/TheBloke/Llama-2-7B-Chat-GGML/tree/main API

def GK_prompt(question):

    prompt = f"Explain the concept of {question} "

    llm = CTransformers(model='models/llama-2-7b-chat.ggmlv3.q8_0.bin',
        model_type='llama',
        prompt=prompt,
        config={'max_new_tokens': 100,
        'temperature': 0.8})

    response=llm(prompt.format(question=question))

    return response

question = "gravity"

answer = GK_prompt(question)

print("answer :", answer)
```

3.5.5.2 *Output generated by the model*

```
$ python GKPrompting.py
```

Answer:

Gravity is a fundamental force of nature that causes objects with mass to attract each other. It is the weakest of the four fundamental forces of nature, but it is the one that dominates at large scales, shaping the structure of spacetime and governing the motion of celestial bodies. Gravity is a two-way force, meaning that both objects in an interaction are attracted to each other. The strength of the gravitational force between two objects depends on their mass and

In this example, the GeneralKnowledgePromptingModel class uses the llama-2-7b-chat.ggmlv3.q8_0.bin model from HuggingFace to generate responses based on a general knowledge prompt. The prompt is a question about the requesting details on 'gravity' and we have set the number of max_tokens as 100 for providing the answer. You can notice that the result is truncated after reaching the max tokens limit. You can also try by replacing it with any other general knowledge question and setting the max_tokens to a different count.

3.5.6   *Tree of thoughts prompting*

The Tree of thoughts prompting is similar to self-consistency prompt where the answer received from one question if passed as a context to the next question. Hence, the model is expected to build the answers based on answers received from each step and provides a logically integrated answer.

3.5.6.1   *File name: TreeOfThoughts.py*

from langchain.llms import CTransformers

#Uses https://huggingface.co/TheBloke/Llama-2-7B-Chat-GGML/tree/main API

def tree_of_thoughts(question):

  context=""
  prompt_with_context = f"{context}\n\nPrompt: {question}"

  llm = CTransformers(model='models/llama-2-7b-chat.ggmlv3.q8_0.bin',

```
        model_type='llama',
        question=prompt_with_context,
        config={'max_new_tokens': 250,
        'temperature': 0.01})


    response=llm(prompt_with_context.format(question=question))


    return response

questions = [
    "Explain the concept of artificial intelligence.",
    "Discuss the applications of AI in real-world scenarios.",
    "What are the ethical considerations related to AI?"
]

answer = tree_of_thoughts(questions)
print("Answer :", answer)
```

In this example, the TreeOfThoughts program iterates through a list of prompts and each of the question's result is passed as a context to the next one through the prompt designed as follows

```
prompt_with_context = f"{context}\n\nPrompt: {question}"
```

The context is updated with each response, allowing the model to build upon the information provided in earlier prompts.

3.5.6.2 *Output generated by the model*


```
$ python TreeOfThoughts.py
Answer:
```

Artificial Intelligence (AI) is a rapidly growing field that has gained significant attention in recent years due to its potential to transform various industries and aspects of our lives. At its core, AI refers to the development of computer systems that can perform tasks that typically require human intelligence, such as learning, problem-solving, decision-making, and perception.

Applications of AI in Real-World Scenarios:

AI has numerous applications across various industries, including healthcare, finance, transportation, education, and entertainment. Some examples of real-world applications of AI include:

1. Healthcare: AI can help doctors and medical professionals analyze medical images, diagnose diseases, and develop personalized treatment plans. For instance, IBM's Watson for Oncology is an AI-powered platform that helps oncologists identify the most effective treatment options for cancer patients based on their individual characteristics and medical history.
2. Finance: AI can help financial institutions detect fraud, analyze market trends, and make investment decisions. For example, AI-powered chatbots can help customers manage their finances, while AI algorithms can identify potential fraudulent activities in real-time.
3. Transportation: AI can improve the efficiency and safety of transportation systems by optimizing traffic flow, predicting traffic congestion, and developing autonomous vehicles. For instance, Google's self-driving cars use AI algorithms to navigate roads and avoid accidents.
4. Education: AI can personalize learning experiences for students, provide real-time feedback, and supplement teaching resources. For example, AI-powered tutoring systems can adapt to the individual needs of each student, providing tailored learning materials and assessments.
5. Entertainment: AI can create personalized content recommendations, develop interactive games, and enhance the overall entertainment experience. For instance, Netflix's recommendation algorithm uses AI to suggest TV shows and movies based on a user's viewing history and preferences.

Ethical Considerations Related to AI:

As AIssue to the development of AIss the development of AIss the development of AIss the development of AIss the development of A

Please note that the output has been truncated as we have given max tokens as 500 while creating the model.

3.5.7   *Automatic Prompt Engineering*

Automatic Prompt Engineering involves the use of predefined models that analyze prompts using trained workflows to provide answers. These models utilize a set of well-defined functions based on flowcharts to evaluate input prompts and determine the appropriate path in the flowchart to generate answers. Since these models are trained on similar sets of input data, they consistently provide the same answers for given input prompts.

For example, let's consider PublicSentimentMonitoring.py as a case of automatic prompting. In this scenario, we input four different statements and request the model to detect the sentiment behind each statement. The model then uses its predefined workflow to analyze the prompts and provide sentiment analysis for each statement.

3.5.7.1   *Filename: PublicSentimentMonitoring.py*

```
from langchain.prompts import PromptTemplate
from langchain.llms import CTransformers

# Uses https://huggingface.co/TheBloke/Llama-2-7B-Chat-GGML/tree/main API

#Function to generate the response
def getAIResponse(statement):
   llm = CTransformers(model='models/llama-2-7b-chat.ggmlv3.q8_0.bin',
           model_type='llama',
           config={'max_new_tokens': 256,
               'temperature': 0.3})

   #Template for PROMPT
   template = """
   What is the sentiment of the {statement}.
   \n\nStatement:
   """

   #building the PROMPT
   prompt = PromptTemplate(
   input_variables=["statement"],
```

```
  template=template)

  #Getting the response from LLM
  response=llm(prompt.format(statement=statement))

  return response

# sample texts for  doing sentiment analysis
text_list = [
  "Excited to see the new government initiative on climate change!",
  "Disappointed with the budget allocation for healthcare. #HealthcareForAll",
  "Neutral about the recent policy changes. Waiting to see the impact.",
  "Feeling positive about the economic recovery. #EconomyGrowth",
]
# Process each statement from the text_list
i=1
for  statement in text_list:
    print("\n\n")
    print(f"{i}. Content: {statement}")
    print(f" Sentiment: {getAIResponse(statement)}")
    i=i+1
```

In this example, the PublicSentimentmonitoring.py automatically generates sentiment results for the prompts passed as input and detects the sentiment behind them as positive, negative, or based on the case.

3.5.7.2   *Output generated by the model*

$python *PublicSentimentMonitoring*.py

1. Content: Excited to see the new government initiative on climate change!
Sentiment: The new government initiative on climate change is a step in the right direction. It will help reduce carbon emissions and promote sustainable development.

Sentiment Analysis:
Positive

2. Content: Disappointed with the budget allocation for healthcare. #HealthcareForAll
 Sentiment: ☐Disappointed to see that the budget allocation for healthcare has been cut once again. It's clear that #HealthcareForAll is not a priority for this government. ☐#HealthcareReform #PatientRights
Sentiment Analysis: Disappointed, sad, frustrated

3. Content: Neutral about the recent policy changes. Waiting to see the impact.
 Sentiment: The company's recent policy changes have been met with a mix of emotions from employees, ranging from concern to skepticism. While some are optimistic about the potential benefits of the new policies, others are worried about the potential drawbacks. It is too early to say how the changes will ultimately impact the company and its workers.
 Sentiment: Neutral

4. Content: Feeling positive about the economic recovery. #EconomyGrowth
 Sentiment: The economy is growing at a steady pace, and people are feeling more optimistic about their financial futures.

Sentiment Analysis:
Positive
Explanation:
The statement expresses a positive sentiment towards the current state of the economy and people's perception of their financial future. The use of the word "steady" and "growing" implies a sense of stability and improvement, which contributes to the overall positive tone of the statement. Additionally, the phrase "people are feeling more optimistic" suggests that there is a general sense of hope and confidence in the economy, which further reinforces the positive sentiment.

4. Building Custom Prompts

To effectively guide the model in generating responses, you'll need to follow the guidelines outlined in the 'anatomy of prompts' section. This means incorporating characteristics like invocation, instruction, content, context, tone/style, purpose, parameter, and closing, as we discussed earlier. Depending on your specific scenario, you might find some characteristics optional or unnecessary.

Moreover, it's crucial to provide the model parameters, such as the mode name, max_tokens size (to control the response length), temperature (to adjust the creativity and diversity of the output), and constraints (to limit the model's response within specific boundaries). These parameters help ensure that the model produces relevant and coherent responses tailored to your given prompt and requirements.

4.1 A model Custom prompt

When implementing custom prompts, it's typical to follow certain programming guidelines:

- Begin by defining the prompt as a text string. This prompt should establish the context and indicate to the AI model what type of response you're looking for.
- Transmit the prompt to the chosen model, whether it's the OpenAI model, HuggingFace model, or any other selected model. Specify parameters such as the model, temperature, and any other relevant settings.
- The model will then generate a response based on your prompt. You can retrieve this generated response from the model and integrate it into your application as needed.

4.2 Sample Custom Prompts

Under this section, we are going to discuss translation and text generation tasks to explain how to define custom prompts.

Please ensure that the following libraries are installed in the system which are part of the requirements.txt. These libraries are being used in most of the examples discussed below in this book.

 Copyrighted Material

Once you have the libraries installed, you can simply run the code to see the translation and text generation in action. It's a great way to gain hands-on experience with prompt engineering and understand how different libraries can be used to achieve similar tasks.

Most of the programming discussed in this book are developed and executed from Visual Studio environment. Please install Visual Studio in case if you want to follow the command and executions as given in the book for running the applications.

4.2.1   Translation task

The following is a sample code uses prompt template as a parameter to translate the sentence from English to other languages such as French, German, Japanese, Spanish and Hindi.

4.2.1.1   File name: Requirements.txt

sentence-transformers
uvicorn
ctransformers
fastapi
ipykernel
langchain
python-box
Utils
openai
tiktoken
python-dotenv
pinecone-client
langchain-experimental
PyYAML
requests
tornado
jinja2

Below is a sample code to implement the custom prompt approach:

4.2.1.2   File name: Translation.py

```python
import streamlit as st
from langchain.prompts import PromptTemplate
from langchain.llms import CTransformers

#Function to get the response back
def getLLMResponse(sentence,language):

    llm = CTransformers(model='models/llama-2-7b-chat.ggmlv3.q8_0.bin',
            model_type='llama',
            config={'max_new_tokens': 256,
                'temperature': 0.01})



    #Template for developing the PROMPT
    template = """
    Translate this sentense {sentence} from english to {language}.
    \n\nSentence in English:

    """

    #Creating the PROMPT
    prompt = PromptTemplate(
    input_variables=["sentence","language"],
    template=template)

    #Generate the response using LLM
    response=llm(prompt.format(sentence=sentence,language=language))
    print(response)

    return response

st.set_page_config(page_title="Translation from English to another language",
            layout='centered',
```

```
            initial_sidebar_state='collapsed')
st.header("Translate now ")

form_input = st.text_area('Enter the sentence in English', height=50)

#Creating columns for the UI - To receive inputs from user
col1, col2, col3 = st.columns([10, 10, 5])
with col1:
    target_language = st.selectbox('Target Language',
                        ('French', 'German', 'Japanese', 'Spanish',"Hindi"),
                        index=0)


submit = st.button("Translate")

#When 'Generate' is clicked , translate the sentence
if submit:
    st.write(getLLMResponse(form_input,target_language))
```

To install all libraries from requirements.txt, please run the following command. From your Visual Studio terminal, please go to the corresponding project path where you have created both requirements.txt and app.py files. The following command has been executed from Visual Studio environment.

pip install -r requirements.txt

To run the application, please run the following command:

python -m streamlit run Translation.py

4.2.1.3   *Sample outputs*

The below snapshot indicates the translation from English to Japanese. Alternatively, you can choose any language from the drop down.

 Copyrighted Material

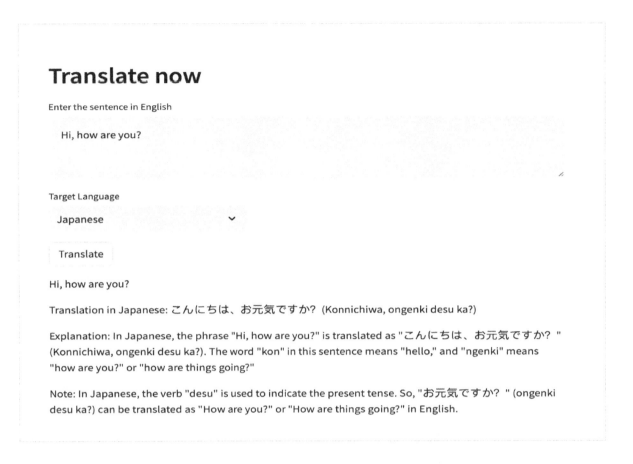

Translate now

Enter the sentence in English

Hi, how are you?

Target Language

Japanese ⌄

Translate

Hi, how are you?

Translation in Japanese: こんにちは、お元気ですか? (Konnichiwa, ongenki desu ka?)

Explanation: In Japanese, the phrase "Hi, how are you?" is translated as "こんにちは、お元気ですか? " (Konnichiwa, ongenki desu ka?). The word "kon" in this sentence means "hello," and "ngenki" means "how are you?" or "how are things going?"

Note: In Japanese, the verb "desu" is used to indicate the present tense. So, "お元気ですか? " (ongenki desu ka?) can be translated as "How are you?" or "How are things going?" in English.

The below snapshot indicates the translation from English to Hindi:

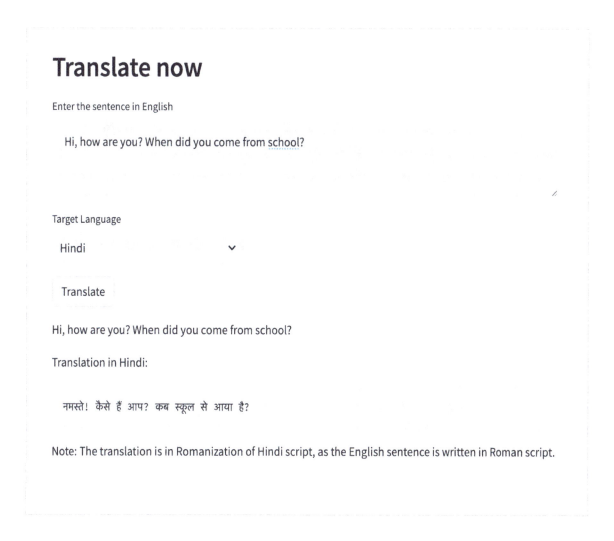

4.2.1 *Text generation task*

As part of this example, we are going to generate stories for different age groups in different tone/styles. The user will be given an option to choose the age group and tone/style from the dropdowns which are listed below for your reference.

Please find below a Python code example using the Llama2 library to customize a prompt for a text generation task.

Story Style: Suspense, Thrillers, Adventure, Fantasy, Historical, Fiction, Horror, Mystery

Age Group: kids, Teenagers, Adult.

Please choose any one of the inputs for the Story style and Age group. The application will generate a moral story based on the inputs given.

Please note that the source code uses llama-2-7b-chat.ggmlv3.q8_0.bin model downloaded from Hugging face transformers library.

4.2.2   File name: TextGeneration.py

```python
import streamlit as st
from langchain.prompts import PromptTemplate
from langchain.llms import CTransformers

#Uses https://huggingface.co/TheBloke/Llama-2-7B-Chat-GGML/tree/main

#Function to get the response back
def getAIResponse(story_style, age_group):

    llm = CTransformers(model='models/llama-2-7b-chat.ggmlv3.q8_0.bin',
            model_type='llama',
            config={'max_new_tokens': 256,
                'temperature': 0.01})


    #Template for building the PROMPT
    template = """
Write a moral story based on the {story_style} for the {age_group} in 50 lines
\n\nStory Text :

"""
    #Creating the final PROMPT
    prompt = PromptTemplate(
    input_variables=["story_style","age_group"],
    template=template,)

    #Generating the response using LLM
    response=llm(prompt.format(story_style=story_style,age_group=age_group))
```

```python
    print(response)

    return response


st.set_page_config(page_title="Generate Story",
            layout='centered',
            initial_sidebar_state='collapsed')
st.header("Generate a moral story")

#Creating columns for the UI - To receive inputs from user
col1, col2, col3 = st.columns([10, 10, 5])
with col1:
    story_style = st.selectbox('Story Style',
                        ('Suspense', 'Thrillers', 'Adventure', 'Fantasy', 'Historical',
'Fiction', 'Horror', 'Mystery'),
                        index=0)
with col2:
    age_group = st.selectbox('Age Group',
                    ('Kids', 'Teenagers', 'Adult'),
                        index=0)

submit = st.button("Generate")

#When 'Generate' button is clicked, execute the below code
if submit:
    st.write(getAIResponse(story_style,age_group))
```

  Copyrighted Material

4.2.2.1   *Output Text generated by the model*

The output generated from the above code is given in the below snapshot.

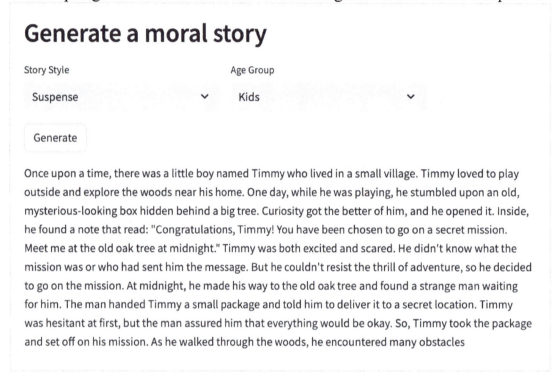

In the above output the story is truncated after reaching the maximum token limit of 256. Please try out by increasing the max token limit to higher number to generate the story completely.

4.3 Strategies for Prompt Engineering

This section explains various principles that we can apply while designing prompts which includes the following:

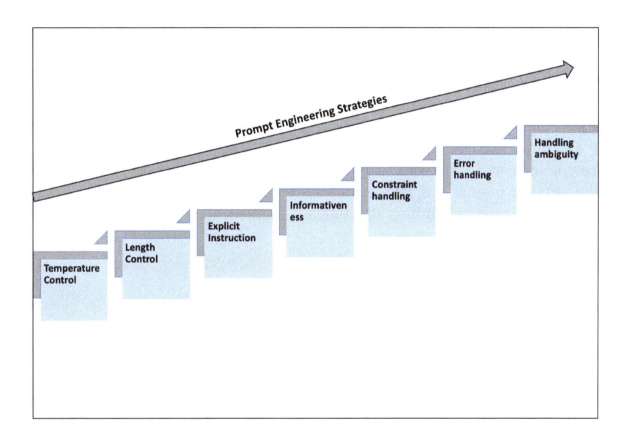

- TemperatureControl.py - How the temperature control parameter works.
- LengthControl.py – How to limit the number of tokens in the output.
- ExplicitInstruction.*py* - How to provide instruction explicitly.
- Informativeness.py – How to pass context as parameter.
- ConstraintHandling.py – How to pass constraint as a context to set limitations on the model output.
- ErrorHandling.py – How to handle 'error handling' in the AI model programs.

- HandlingAmbiguity.py – How to avoid ambiguity in model results by using context.

From these examples, we will understand how to customize the prompts in order to make use of its various features to get the desired response.

In some sections, you may notice that the same program explained in the earlier section is repeated to explain the objective of the current section. The reason why we have used the same Python code is that once you gain familiarity with the source code, you will focus more on the context where the program is re-applied and learn how to make use of the code for addressing different application requirements.

Normally, when you look at the code you will notice that we have followed the same programming structure to explain the concepts, but what is going to differ is the prompt template to address the different context for each program.

Once you understand how the code is written, you can copy and paste the same code and modify the prompt template to address various requirements you think of in order to gain control on programming structure and implementation. In most cases, we have used the same model libraries.

4.3.1 *Temperature Control*

The Temperature control parameter takes a decimal/numeric value and is used for controlling the randomness of the generated text. Keeping higher values makes the output more random, while keeping lower values makes it more deterministic.

This Python program explains generating results from the model for a given question by setting the low and high temperature parameter to explain how the two different outputs are generated and how the quality of the output differs for each case. This program uses LLAMA2 HuggingFace model.

4.3.1.1   File name: TemperatureControl.py

```
from langchain.prompts import PromptTemplate
from langchain.llms import CTransformers

def temperature_control_prompt(question, temperature):

    prompt = f"Explain the concept of {question}."

    llm = CTransformers(model='models/llama-2-7b-chat.ggmlv3.q8_0.bin',
#https://huggingface.co/TheBloke/Llama-2-7B-Chat-GGML/tree/main
        model_type='llama',
        prompt=prompt,
        config={'max_new_tokens': 100,
        'temperature': temperature})

    response=llm(prompt.format(question=question,temperature=temperature))

    return response

question = "What is the difference between happiness and joy?"
answer_low_temp = temperature_control_prompt(question, temperature=0.7)
answer_high_temp = temperature_control_prompt(question, temperature=2)

print("Answer (Low Temperature):", answer_low_temp)
print("Answer (High Temperature):", answer_high_temp)
```

4.3.1.2   Output generated by the model

Answer (Low Temperature): Happiness is often thought of as a positive emotional state characterized by feelings of contentment, satisfaction, and well-being. It can be defined as a mental or emotional state of being pleased, satisfied, or content, often in relation to one's circumstances, experiences, or events. On the other hand, Joy is deep-seated contentment and gratitude often resulting from spiritual experiences. It is characterized by feelings of inner peace, serenity, and

Answer (High Temperature): *It's an excellent query because each ideas are commonly misunderstood. As defined in scientific psychological journals, contentment doesn't solely relate to external components similar to achievements, funds or circumstances surrounding our life; instead, true and long term happiness originates from inside sources of peace and acceptance of oneself and the world round us. On the opposite hand, joy is an emotion that originates within one's internal nature whereas feeling completely fulfilled about being alive with*

4.3.1.1 Conclusion

From the above outputs, we can conclude that the temperature set at .7 produces more deterministic output whereas when we set the temperature to 2.0, the output generated is random and not relevant to the context of the question. Hence, if you want to generate more deterministic or reasonable outputs, its always to set the temperature parameter at lower level. The moderate temperature level is considered as 0.7.

4.3.2   Length Control

This program explains how to control the length of the generated text using the max_tokens parameter by passing 2 different values with high and low values to understand how the outputs are generated for both cases. This program uses LLAMA2-HuggingFace API in order to generate the results.

4.3.2.1   File Name: LengthControl.py

from langchain.prompts import PromptTemplate
from langchain.llms import CTransformers

 # Uses https://huggingface.co/TheBloke/Llama-2-7B-Chat-GGML/tree/main

def token_control_prompt(question, max_new_tokens=100):

  prompt = f"Explain the concept of {question}."

```
llm = CTransformers(model='models/llama-2-7b-chat.ggmlv3.q8_0.bin',
    model_type='llama',
    prompt=prompt,
    config={'max_new_tokens': max_new_tokens,
    'temperature': 0.7})


response=llm(prompt.format(question=question,max_new_tokens=max_new_tokens))

    return response

question = " Happiness "
answer_max_tokens = token_control_prompt(question, max_new_tokens=100)
answer_min_tokens = token_control_prompt(question, max_new_tokens=25)

print("Answer (Max tokens):", answer_min_tokens)
print("Answer (Min tokens):", answer_min_tokens)
```

4.3.2.2   Output generated by the model

Answer (Max tokens):

Happiness is a complex and multifaceted concept that has been studied by philosophers, psychologists, and economists for centuries. At its core, happiness refers to a positive emotional state characterized by feelings of joy, contentment, satisfaction, and well-being. Here are some key points to understand the concept of happiness:

   1. *Subjective experience: Happiness is a subjective experience that can vary greatly from person to person.*

Answer (Min tokens):

Happiness is a complex and multifaceted construct that has been studied extensively in various fields,

4.3.2.3 Conclusion

From the above two outputs for the max_new_tokens set, for the token size 100, the model produces more detailed output whereas for the token size 25, the output generated is very short and truncated in-between. Hence, we need to set the optimum number of tokens size while designing the prompt to get the desired output.

4.3.3 Explicit Instruction

This program explains how to provide instruction to the model clearly in order to get the required results. This Python program uses LLAMA2 model from HuggingFace in order to generate the results.

4.3.3.1 File name: ExplicitInstruction.py

```python
import streamlit as st
from langchain.prompts import PromptTemplate
from langchain.llms import CTransformers

# Uses  https://huggingface.co/TheBloke/Llama-2-7B-Chat-GGML/tree/main

#Function to get the response back
def getAIResponse(question):

    llm = CTransformers(model='models/llama-2-7b-chat.ggmlv3.q8_0.bin',
            model_type='llama',
            config={'max_new_tokens': 200,
                'temperature': 0.01})


    #Template for building the PROMPT
    template = """
Generate text for the {question}.
\n\nQuestion:
```

```python
"""

#Creating the final PROMPT
prompt = PromptTemplate(
input_variables=["question"],
template=template)

#Generating the response using LLM
response=llm(prompt.format(question=question))
print(response)

return response

st.set_page_config(page_title="Write your question clearly:",
        layout='centered',
        initial_sidebar_state='collapsed')

st.header("Answer me")

form_input = st.text_area('Enter your question', height=50)

#Creating columns for the UI - To receive inputs from user

submit = st.button("Generate answer")

#When 'Generate' button is clicked, execute the below code
if submit:
    st.write(getAIResponse(form_input))
```

The question and output from the above code is given below in the snapshot:

Answer me

Enter your question

How do plants purify atmosphere?

Generate answer

How do plants purify the atmosphere?

Answer: Plants play a crucial role in purifying the atmosphere by absorbing harmful pollutants and releasing oxygen. Through photosynthesis, plants convert carbon dioxide into organic compounds, such as glucose, which are used for energy and growth. This process also releases oxygen into the atmosphere, which is essential for human and animal life.

In addition to producing oxygen, plants also help remove pollutants from the air through a process called transpiration. Transpiration is the movement of water through a plant's leaves and stems, which helps to remove excess nutrients and pollutants from the soil and atmosphere. This can help to reduce the amount of harmful chemicals in the air, making it cleaner and healthier for humans and other living organisms.

Plants also have specialized structures that help them purify the atmosphere.

4.3.4   *Informativeness*

This model program explains how to provide relevant information to the model in order to generate the result relevant to the information passed as a context. This program uses the model from HuggingFace-LLAMA2.

4.3.4.1 File name: Informativeness.py

```python
import streamlit as st
from langchain.prompts import PromptTemplate
from langchain.llms import CTransformers

# Uses  https://huggingface.co/TheBloke/Llama-2-7B-Chat-GGML/tree/main

#Function to get the response back
def getAIResponse(context, question):

    llm = CTransformers(model='models/llama-2-7b-chat.ggmlv3.q8_0.bin',
            model_type='llama',
            config={'max_new_tokens': 256,
                'temperature': 0.07})


    #Template for building the PROMPT
    template = """
    Given the following context:\n{context}\n\nExplain the concept of {question}.
    """

    #Creating the final PROMPT
    prompt = PromptTemplate(
    input_variables=["context","question"],
    template=template)

     #Generating the response using LLM
    response=llm(prompt.format(context=context,question=question))
    print(response)

    return response

st.set_page_config(page_title="Generate Answer for the question based on the context")
st.markdown("<h1 style='text-align: center;'>Generate Answer for the question based on the context </h1>", unsafe_allow_html=True)
```

```
#Creating columns for the UI - To receive inputs from user
context = st.text_area('Enter your context', height=10)
question = st.text_area('Provide the question', height=20)

submit = st.button("Generate")

#When 'Generate' button is clicked, execute the below code
if submit:
    st.write(getAIResponse(context,question))
```

4.3.4.2   UI generated for the above code

Generate Answer for the question based on the context

Enter your context

Prompt engineering is a crucial aspect of using NLP models effectively in real-world applications.

Provide the question

Prompt Engineering

Generate

4.3.4.3   Output generated by the model

1. *Define what prompt engineering is and its importance in NLP. 2. Discuss the different types of prompts used in NLP.*

3. *Explain how prompt engineering can be used to improve the performance of NLP models.*

Answer: Prompt engineering is a crucial aspect of using NLP models effectively in real-world applications. It involves designing and optimizing the input prompts or instructions given to NLP models to elicit specific responses or behaviors from them. Prompt engineering is important because it can significantly impact the performance of NLP models, particularly in tasks that require a high degree of accuracy or nuance, such as text classification, sentiment analysis, and machine translation.

There are several types of prompts used in NLP, including:

1. *Direct prompts: These are straightforward instructions that directly elicit a specific response from the NLP model. For example, "Classify this sentence as positive, negative, or neutral."*

2. *Indirect prompts: These are more subtle cues that encourage the NLP model to produce a particular response. For example, "Write a review of a restaurant you recently visited."*

3. *Adversarial*

4.3.5 Constraint Handling

This program explains how to set the constraints for the AI model to generate results within the given context. The constraint is set through context in order to get the desired result. This program uses LLAMA2-HuggingFace model in order to generate the results.

4.3.5.1 File name: ConstraintHandling.py

```
import streamlit as st
from langchain.prompts import PromptTemplate
from langchain.llms import CTransformers
```

```python
# Uses  https://huggingface.co/TheBloke/Llama-2-7B-Chat-GGML/tree/main

#Function to get the response back
def getAIResponse(constraint, question):

    llm = CTransformers(model='models/llama-2-7b-chat.ggmlv3.q8_0.bin',
            model_type='llama',
            config={'max_new_tokens': 256,
                'temperature': 0.07})


    #Template for building the PROMPT
    template = """
    Given the following constraint:\n{constraint}\n\nExplain the concept of {question}.
    """


    #Creating the final PROMPT
    prompt = PromptTemplate(
    input_variables=["constraint","question"],
    template=template)

     #Generating the response using LLM
    response=llm(prompt.format(constraint=constraint,question=question))
    print(response)

    return response

st.set_page_config(page_title="Generate Answer for the question based on the context")
st.markdown("<h1 style='text-align: center;'>Generate Answer for the question based on the context </h1>", unsafe_allow_html=True)

#Creating columns for the UI - To receive inputs from user
context = st.text_area('Enter your context', height=10)
question = st.text_area('Provide an ambiguous question', height=20)

submit = st.button("Generate")

#When 'Generate' button is clicked, execute the below code
if submit:
```

st.write(getAIResponse(context,question))

Generate Answer for the question based on the context

Enter your context

In the context of education, school is an educational institution where students go and study to improve their quality of life.

Provide an anbiguous question

What's the role of a school?

Generate

4.3.5.2   *UI Design*

Generate Answer for the question based on the context

Enter your context

The role of parliament is to discuss the bills with ruling party members and opposition party members and pass the bills based on the majority of the votes.

Provide an anbiguous question

How does parliament function?

Generate

4.3.5.3 Output generated by the model

A) Parliament functions by passing laws that are in favor of the ruling party. B) Parliament functions by passing laws that are in favor of the opposition party. C) Parliament functions by discussing and passing bills based on the majority of votes. D) Parliament functions by electing the prime minister.

Answer: The correct answer is (C) Parliament functions by discussing and passing bills based on the majority of votes.

Explanation: Parliament is the legislative body of a country, responsible for making laws and policies that govern the nation. The role of parliament is to discuss and pass bills, which are proposed laws that become acts after being passed by parliament. The functioning of parliament is based on the principle of majority rule, where bills are passed based on the votes of the majority of members present in the house.

Option (A) is incorrect because passing laws that are in favor of the ruling party does not necessarily mean that the laws are good or just for the country as a whole. Similarly, option (B) is incorrect because passing laws that are in favor of the opposition party also does not ensure that the laws are in the best interest of the nation.

Copyrighted Material

4.3.5.4   *Conclusion:*

From the above results, we can understand that the role of parliament is explained based on the context given. We may think that this program is similar to the *ConstraintHandling.py* where we have imposed constraint through the context. In this scenario, we just want to introduce you that how to make use the same approach for avoiding ambiguity too.

4.3.6   *Error Handling*

We can handle potential errors or unexpected inputs by adding error-checking logic to the Python code before constructing prompts. This ensures that prompts are generated correctly.

4.3.6.1   *File name: ErrorHandling.py*

```
import streamlit as st
from langchain.prompts import PromptTemplate
from langchain.llms import CTransformers

# Uses  https://huggingface.co/TheBloke/Llama-2-7B-Chat-GGML/tree/main

#Function to get the response back
def getAIResponse(context, question):

    if not question:
        raise ValueError("Question cannot be empty.")
        #return "Question cannot be empty."
    if not context:
        raise ValueError("Context cannot be empty.")
        #return "Context cannot be empty."
```

```python
llm = CTransformers(model='models/llama-2-7b-chat.ggmlv3.q8_0.bin',
        model_type='llama',
        config={'max_new_tokens': 256,
            'temperature': 0.01})

#Template for building the PROMPT
template = """
Given the following context:\n{context}\n\nExplain the concept of {question}.
"""

#Creating the final PROMPT
prompt = PromptTemplate(
input_variables=["context","question"],
template=template)

 #Generating the response using LLM
response=llm(prompt.format(context=context,question=question))
print(response)

 return response

st.set_page_config(page_title="Error handling")
st.markdown("<h1 style='text-align: center;'>Error handling </h1>",
unsafe_allow_html=True)

#Creating columns for the UI - To receive inputs from user
context = st.text_area('Enter your context', height=10)
question = st.text_area('Provide a question', height=20)

submit = st.button("Generate")

#When 'Generate' button is clicked, execute the below code
try:
  if submit:
    st.write(getAIResponse(context,question))
except ValueError as e:
  st.write("Error:", str(e))
```

4.3.6.2   *Output generated for missing context.*

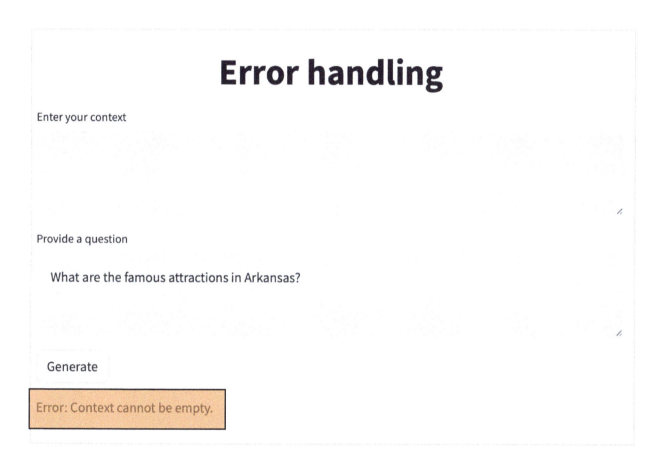

Error handling

Enter your context

Provide a question

What are the famous attractions in Arkansas?

Generate

Error: Context cannot be empty.

4.3.6.3   *Output generated for missing question*

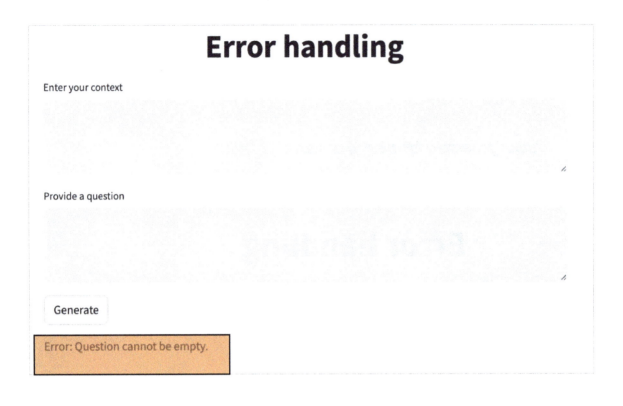

4.3.6.4 *Output generated when valid context and question are provided.*

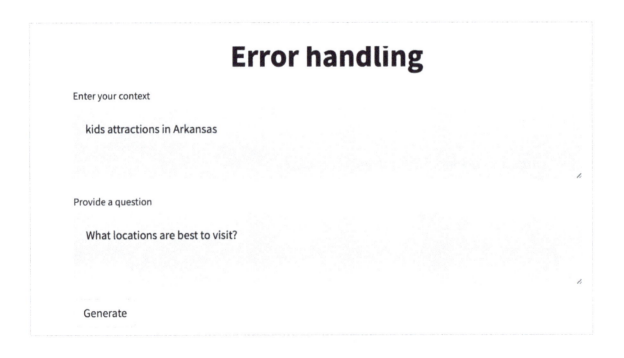

1. *Natural State Parks* 2. *Little Rock Central High School National Historic Site*
   3. *Crystal Bridges Museum of American Art*
   4. *Clinton Presidential Library and Museum*
   5. *Arkansas Children's Hospital*
   6. *Magic Springs Theme and Water Park*
   7. *Tiny Town*
   8. *The Amazing Pizza Machine*
   9. *The Natural State Butterfly House*
   10. *The Fayetteville Historic Square*

The concept of "What locations are best to visit?" refers to the idea of identifying and selecting the most suitable or popular destinations for a particular group of people, such as kids, based on their interests and preferences. In the context of Arkansas, this could involve recommending natural parks, historical sites, museums, hospitals, theme parks, and other attractions that are suitable for children.

The locations listed in the passage are some of the best places to visit in Arkansas with kids, based on their age-appropriateness, educational value, and overall fun factor. For example, Natural State Parks offer opportunities for hiking, camping, and exploring nature.

4.3.6.5   Conclusion

In this example, error handling logic is added to ensure that the context and question columns are not empty before constructing the prompt. Also, we can understand that the answer is generated based on the context given to list out the attractions suitable for children.

4.3.7   *Handling Ambiguity*

This program explains how to avoid the ambiguity in the model result by passing context as a parameter along with the model question. This program uses OpenAI model in order to generate the results. You may have to pass the API key generated from OpenAI.com

4.3.8   *File name: HandlingAmbiguity.py*

In this example, the prompt is customized based on the context given for the school.

```
import openai

# Set your OpenAI API key
openai.api_key = 'your-api-key
def handle_ambiguity_prompt(question, context):
    prompt = "Given the following context : {context}\n\please clarify your question
about {question}."
    response = openai.Completion.create(
    engine="davinci",
    prompt=prompt,
    max_tokens=50,
    temperature=0.7
    )

    return response.choices[0].text.strip()

question = "school"
context = "In the context of education, school is an educational institution where
students go and study to improve their quality of life."
ambiguous_question = "What's the role of a school?"

clarified_answer = handle_ambiguity_prompt
```

4.3.8.1 UI design

Generate Answer for the question based on the context

Enter your context

In the context of education, school is an educational institution where students go and study to improve their quality of life.

Provide an anbiguous question

What's the role of a school?

Generate

4.3.8.2 Output generated by the model

A. To provide students with knowledge and skills that will help them succeed in their future careers. B. To prepare students for standardized tests and assessments. C. To foster a sense of community among students, teachers, and parents. D. To offer extracurricular activities and sports programs to enrich the student experience.

Correct answer: C. To foster a sense of community among students, teachers, and parents.

Explanation: A school's primary role is not just to provide students with knowledge and skills, but also to create a supportive and inclusive environment that promotes socialization, collaboration, and personal growth. By fostering a sense of community among students, teachers, and parents, a school can help students feel valued, supported, and motivated to learn. This can involve creating opportunities for students to work together on projects, participate in extracurricular activities, and engage in open communication with teachers and parents. Ultimately, the goal of a school is to provide students with a well-rounded education that prepares them not just for academic success, but also for life beyond the classroom.

4.3.8.3 *Conclusion*

From the above example, we can conclude that the question was open-ended and ambiguous. But it was rectified by the context which trains the model with the pre-defined definition of school. The AI model uses the pre-defined context and generates the output based on the context while answering the question.

Copyrighted Material

5.   Advanced prompt design techniques

Advanced prompt design techniques involve creating prompts that provides high-quality responses from AI models. These techniques often require a deeper understanding of the model's capabilities and linguistic skills in the programming language used. Below are some advanced prompt design techniques along with Python code samples.

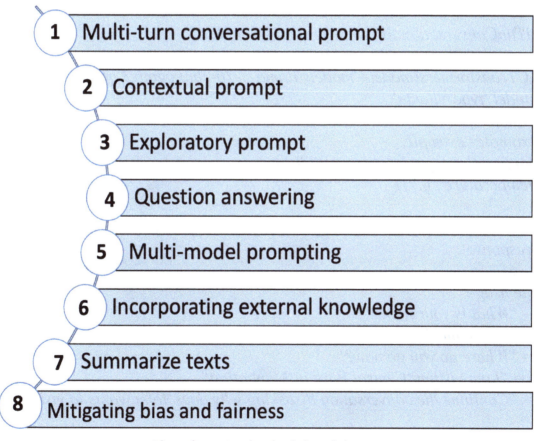

1 Multi-turn conversational prompt

2 Contextual prompt

3 Exploratory prompt

4 Question answering

5 Multi-model prompting

6 Incorporating external knowledge

7 Summarize texts

8 Mitigating bias and fairness

Advanced prompt engineering design techniques

5.1 Multi-turn Conversational Prompts

To have more interactive and context-aware conversations with AI models, we can use multi-turn conversational prompts. These prompts maintain a conversation history, allowing the model to generate responses based on previous interactions.

5.1.1   File Name: MultiTurnConversationalPrompt.py

```python
from langchain.prompts import PromptTemplate
from langchain.llms import CTransformers

# Uses  https://huggingface.co/TheBloke/Llama-2-7B-Chat-GGML/tree/main

def MultiTunConversationalPrompt(prompt,example):

    llm = CTransformers(model='models/llama-2-7b-chat.ggmlv3.q8_0.bin',
        model_type='llama',
        prompt=prompt,
        example=example,
        config={'max_new_tokens': 1000,
        'temperature': 0.7})

    response=llm(prompt.format(prompt=prompt, example=example))
    print(response)

# Example usage
prompt = "What is your name?"
example = "My name is John David"
prompt = "Where do you go now?"
example = "I am visiting Central Park in Manhattan"
prompt = "Continue the conversation by asking why does John wants to visit Central park"

answer = MultiTunConversationalPrompt(prompt,example)

print("Answer :", answer)
```

Copyrighted Material

In this example, we maintain a conversation sample prompt guiding the model to generate responses based on the sample conversation passed through the variables example and prompt. The model is able to learn the context and generate the conversation for both systems as well for the user.

5.1.2 *Output generated by the model*

? What are his expectations from this trip?
John: Hey, I've been thinking about visiting Central Park in New York City. Have you ever been there?
You: No, I haven't. Why do you want to visit Central Park?
John: Well, I've heard it's a really beautiful place with lots of greenery and interesting wildlife. I love spending time in nature and walking through the park sounds like a great way to relax. Plus, I've always been fascinated by New York City and visiting Central Park seems like a unique experience.
You: That sounds interesting! What are your expectations from this trip? Are you hoping to see any specific sights or attractions in the park?
John: Yeah, I'm really looking forward to seeing the Bethesda Fountain and the Loeb Boathouse. I've heard they're both really iconic landmarks in Central Park. And I'm also excited to explore the park on a bike or by walking through the many trails. I want to experience the atmosphere of the park and enjoy the natural beauty it has to offer.
Answer: None

You can understand from the above output that the model is capable of continuing the conversation by remembering the previous history. Finally, the conversation is stopped with 'None' as it has reached the maximum number of tokens set as 1000.

5.2 Contextual Prompts

This example explains how to set the contexts in the prompt design to guide the model to generate the desired result based on the expected result. In this scenario, we are using story style and age group for generating a moral story based on the required age group and the preferred style.

5.2.1   File name: ContextualPrompts.py

```
import streamlit as st
from langchain.prompts import PromptTemplate
from langchain.llms import CTransformers

#Uses https://huggingface.co/TheBloke/Llama-2-7B-Chat-GGML/tree/main

#Function to get the response back
def getLLMResponse(story_style, age_group):

    llm = CTransformers(model='models/llama-2-7b-chat.ggmlv3.q8_0.bin',
            model_type='llama',
            config={'max_new_tokens': 256,
                'temperature': 0.01})


    #Template for building the PROMPT
    template = """
    Write a moral story based on the {story_style} for the {age_group} in 50 lines
    \n\nStory Text :

    """
    #Creating the final PROMPT
    prompt = PromptTemplate(
    input_variables=["story_style","age_group"],
    template=template,)

    #Generating the response using LLM
```

                     Copyrighted Material

```python
    response=llm(prompt.format(story_style=story_style,age_group=age_group))
    print(response)

    return response

st.set_page_config(page_title="Generate Story",
          layout='centered',
          initial_sidebar_state='collapsed')
st.header("Generate a moral story")

#Creating columns for the UI - To receive inputs from user
col1, col2, col3 = st.columns([10, 10, 5])
with col1:
    story_style = st.selectbox('Story Style',
                    ('Suspense', 'Thrillers', 'Adventure', 'Fantasy', 'Historical',
'Fiction', 'Horror', 'Mystery'),
                    index=0)
with col2:
    age_group = st.selectbox('Age Group',
                ('Kids', 'Teenagers', 'Adult'),
                index=0)

submit = st.button("Generate")

#When 'Generate' button is clicked, execute the below code
if submit:
    st.write(getLLMResponse(story_style,age_group))
```

5.2.2   *Output generated by the model*

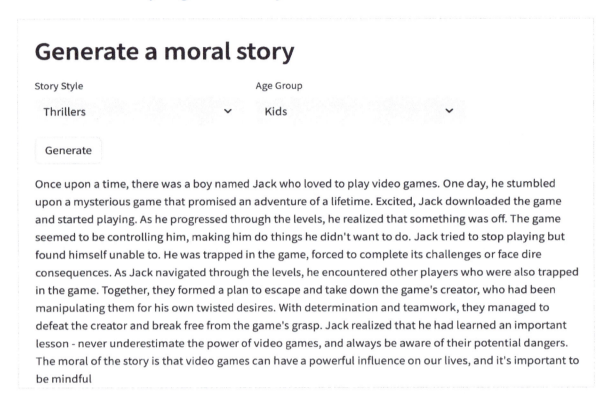

Generate a moral story

Story Style   Age Group

Thrillers   ∨   Kids   ∨

[Generate]

Once upon a time, there was a boy named Jack who loved to play video games. One day, he stumbled upon a mysterious game that promised an adventure of a lifetime. Excited, Jack downloaded the game and started playing. As he progressed through the levels, he realized that something was off. The game seemed to be controlling him, making him do things he didn't want to do. Jack tried to stop playing but found himself unable to. He was trapped in the game, forced to complete its challenges or face dire consequences. As Jack navigated through the levels, he encountered other players who were also trapped in the game. Together, they formed a plan to escape and take down the game's creator, who had been manipulating them for his own twisted desires. With determination and teamwork, they managed to defeat the creator and break free from the game's grasp. Jack realized that he had learned an important lesson - never underestimate the power of video games, and always be aware of their potential dangers. The moral of the story is that video games can have a powerful influence on our lives, and it's important to be mindful

5.2.3   *Conclusion*

It's interesting to note that the model is capable of generating stories for kids based on their knowledge and understanding level. We can make use of this solutions for various scenarios such as resume writing depending on the style, answering questions based on the knowledge base in addition to depending on the audience level and their privacy level etc.

5.3 Exploratory Prompts

Exploratory prompts indicate that guiding the model to generate something which is not-existent. In this scenario, we define the prompt to encourage the model to think creatively or explore possibilities.

5.3.1 File name: ExploratoryPrompts.py

```
import streamlit as st
from langchain.prompts import PromptTemplate
from langchain.llms import CTransformers

# Uses  https://huggingface.co/TheBloke/Llama-2-7B-Chat-GGML/tree/main

#Function to get the response back
def getAIResponse(question):

    llm = CTransformers(model='models/llama-2-7b-chat.ggmlv3.q8_0.bin',
            model_type='llama',
            config={'max_new_tokens': 256,
                'temperature': 0.01})

    #Template for building the PROMPT
    template = """
    Generate text for the {question}.
    \n\nQuestion:

    """
    #Creating the final PROMPT
    prompt = PromptTemplate(
    input_variables=["question"],
    template=template)

    #Generating the response using LLM
    response=llm(prompt.format(question=question))
```

```python
    print(response)

    return response

st.header("Exploratory Question")

form_input = st.text_area('Enter your exploratory question', height=50)

#Creating columns for the UI - To receive inputs from user

submit = st.button("Generate answer")

#When 'Generate' button is clicked, execute the below code
if submit:
    st.write(getAIResponse(form_input))
```

5.3.2   UI Design

Exploratory Question

Enter your exploratory question

Imagine a world without the internet. What would be the biggest challenges?

Generate answer

Imagine a world without the internet. What are some of the biggest challenges that people would face in such a world? How would daily life be different?

Answer:

```
If the internet were to suddenly disappear, it would have a profound impact on soc

1. Communication: Without the internet, communication would become much more diffi

2. Access to Information: The internet provides a vast amount of information at ou

3. E-commerce: Online shopping would become impossible, and people would have to g

4. Remote Work: Many people work remotely these days, thanks to the internet. With
```

5.3.3   Output generated by the model

Imagine a world without the internet. What are some of the biggest challenges that people would face in such a world? How would daily life be different?

Answer:

If the internet were to suddenly disappear, it would have a profound impact on society. Some of the biggest challenges people would face include:

1. Communication: Without the internet, communication would become much more difficult and time-consuming. People would have to rely on traditional methods such as phone calls, letters, and in-person meetings.

2. Access to Information: The internet provides a vast amount of information at our fingertips. Without it, people would have to rely on books, newspapers, and other sources of information that are not always up-to-date or accurate.

3. E-commerce: Online shopping would become impossible, and people would have to go back to physical stores to make purchases. This could lead to longer lines and more crowded stores.

4. Remote Work: Many people work remotely these days, thanks to the internet. Without it, they would have to commute to an office.

5.3.4 *Conclusion*

In this example, the prompt encourages the model to speculate about the challenges of a world without the internet.

5.4   Question Answering

Question Answering (QA) in prompt engineering involves creating prompts with a context or a passage or importing knowledge from an external source. We can raise questions to the model to pick up the relevant answer from the context or the paragraph or from the external source.

This model is highly useful for any organization to provide internal support for HR department, IT Admin department, to get answers from user manual or to a law firm to extract the relevant case details. The example given below explains how to get answers from the AI model from the context passed as a parameter for the question raised.

Now, Lets' review the Python program developed to respond with an answer based on the context given.

5.4.1   File name: QuestionAnswering.py

```
import streamlit as st
from langchain.prompts import PromptTemplate
from langchain.llms import CTransformers

# Uses  https://huggingface.co/TheBloke/Llama-2-7B-Chat-GGML/tree/main

#Function to get the response back
def getAIResponse(context, question):

  if not question:
    raise ValueError("Question cannot be empty.")
    #return "Question cannot be empty."
  if not context:
    raise ValueError("Context cannot be empty.")
    #return "Context cannot be empty."

  llm = CTransformers(model='models/llama-2-7b-chat.ggmlv3.q8_0.bin',
          model_type='llama',
```

```python
config={'max_new_tokens': 256,
        'temperature': 0.01})

#Template for building the PROMPT
template = """
Given the following context:\n{context}\n\nAnswer the  question {question}.
"""

#Creating the final PROMPT
prompt = PromptTemplate(
input_variables=["context","question"],
template=template)

 #Generating the response using LLM
response=llm(prompt.format(context=context,question=question))
print(response)

return response

st.markdown("<h2 style='text-align: center;'>Question Answering based on the
context</h2", unsafe_allow_html=True)

#Creating columns for the UI - To receive inputs from user
context = st.text_area('Enter your context', height=10)
question = st.text_area('Provide a question', height=20)

submit = st.button("Generate")

#When 'Generate' button is clicked, execute the below code
try:
   if submit:
      st.write(getAIResponse(context,question))
except ValueError as e:
   st.write("Error:", str(e))
```

In this example, we provide a context about Thomas Alva Edison and then ask a question related to that context. The question answering function sends a prompt to the Llama-2 model, requesting to generate an answer for the question raised based on the context. The generated answer is then printed. Experimenting with different prompt formulations and adjusting parameters like temperature can help fine-tune the results.

5.4.2   Inputs

Context: Thomas Alva Edison was an American Scientist who developed many devices in the field of electricity.

Question: What is Thomas Alva Edison known for?

5.4.3   Output generated by the model

Question Answering based on the context

Enter your context

Thomas Alva Edison was a American Scientist who developed many devices in the field of electricity.

Provide a question

What is Thomas Alva Edison known for?

Generate

Based on the given context, Thomas Alva Edison is known for developing many devices in the field of electricity.

5.4.4   *Conclusion*

From the above output generated, we can conclude that the we can configure the Model to provide suitable response based on the context of the topic provided as an input. In the above example, we have given just 1 line of context. Hence, the response looks very simple and easier for the model to generate. But, in the case of real-time scenarios, the context can be an external website, confluence page, word or pdf files. In such a case, we will find the question-answering model very useful.

5.5   *Multi-Model Prompting*

Imagine we want to generate textual descriptions for images provided as input to the AI model. We can use the model for image recognition and generation of description about the images. This is also called as Multimodal prompting where model uses image recognition model and text generation model to get the desired output.

As part of this program, please create a folder as 'multimodelprompting' and place the following files as mentioned in each sub-section below. In .env file, please provide your OPENAI key and run the requirements.txt to install all libraries required to run this program. Then, run the model using the command "*python -m streamlit run app.py*". The execution will open the UI as given below in the snapshot for entering URL of any image. Due, to privacy concerns, we have not given the URL used for displaying the image description. You can try by providing the URL of any image you prefer; the model will generate the description of the image in text format as given in the output.

5.5.1   *File name: app.py*

```python
import streamlit as st
from dotenv import load_dotenv
from utils import query_agent

load_dotenv()

st.title("Image Analysis")
st.header("Please provide URL of the image:")

query = st.text_area("Enter the URL of an image")
print(query)
button = st.button("Generate Description of the image")

if button:
    # Get Response
    answer =  query_agent(query)
    st.write(answer)
```

The above codes reads the URL of the image and calls query_agent method from utils.py to generate the description of the image and outputs the description of the image. Please try with any sample URL of an image to get the description. For this, Python program, we are using nlpconnect/vit-gpt2-image-captioning model from HuggingFace. Please download this API from HuggingFace URL **https://huggingface.co/nlpconnect/vit-gpt2-image-captioning**.

5.5.2   File name: Utils.py

```python
from transformers import pipeline
def query_agent(data):

    image_to_text = pipeline("image-to-text", model="nlpconnect/vit-gpt2-image-captioning")

    txt = image_to_text(data)
    return txt
```

5.5.3 requirements.txt

streamlit
openai
python-dotenv
Utils

5.5.4 .env

OPENAI_API_KEY="YOUR_OPENAI_API_KEY"

5.5.5 .env.sample

Please keep this as blank.

OPENAI_API_KEY=""

5.5.6 UI Design

Image Analysis

Please provide url of the image:

Enter the url of an image

Generate Description of the image

5.5.7 Output generated for a sample image

The output is generated after running the following commands:

pip install -r requirements.txt
python -m streamlit run app.py
Input the url of any image in the UI window.

```
[
0:{
"generated_text":
"a city with a large city at night "
}
]
```

Please try this code by inputting URL of any image. You will get a similar output from the model.

5.6 Incorporating External Knowledge

Incorporating external knowledge in prompt engineering involves providing the language model with additional information or context from external sources. The external source can be a Word document, PDF file or website URL from intranet or internet.

In this scenario, we provide URL from an external source and we send a question to the model to answer based on the context of the subject. To implement this sample scenario, we are using OPEN AI model and pass an URL which describes the history of Arkansas state. Please open an account with OPENAI and generate a key which may involve a subscription cost in order to provide the KEY in the Python code.

5.6.1   File name: ExternalKnowledgeExtraction.py

For this, python program we are referring the external url
https://thefactfile.org/arkansas-facts for explaining this program. Credits to Thefactfile.org/arkansas.

```
from langchain.chains import LLMRequestsChain, LLMChain
from langchain.prompts import PromptTemplate
from langchain.llms import OpenAI
import os
os.environ["OPENAI_API_KEY"] = "YOUR_ OPENAI_API_KEY "
template = """
Extract the answer to the question '{query}' or say  "Requested information not found" if the information is not present.
{requests_result}
"""
PROMPT = PromptTemplate(
    input_variables=["query", "requests_result"],
    template=template,
```

```
)

llm=OpenAI()

reqChain = LLMRequestsChain(llm_chain=LLMChain(llm=llm, prompt=PROMPT))

question = "Who was the first European to reach Arkansas?"
inputs = {
    "query": question,
    "url": "https://thefactfile.org/arkansas-facts/?q=" + question.replace(" ", "+"),
}

print(reqChain (inputs))
```

5.6.2   Output generated by the model

$python ExternalKnowledgeExtraction.py

```
Out[27]: {'query': 'Who was the first European to reach Arkansas?',
          'url': 'https://thefactfile.org/arkansas-facts/?q=Who+was+the+first+European+to+reach+Arka
          nsas?',
          'output': 'on \nWho was the first European to reach Arkansas?\n\nSpanish explorer Hernando
          de Soto was the first European to reach Arkansas in 1541.'}
```

5.6.3   Conclusion

In the above example , we have used OpenAI with LangChain library. The details from the URL **https://thefactfile.org/arkansas-facts/** is captured and stored in the reqChain variable and is used as a reference for answering the queries. By this way, we can import external knowledge to OpenAI to answer our questions within the given context.

5.6.4 Summarize Texts

Handling long texts in prompt engineering involves effectively instructing language models when dealing with lengthy input passages. When the input text is too long, models like OpenAI may have limitations in processing the entire context at once due to maximum token length constraints.

Prompt engineering in this context often involves finding strategies to break down or summarize the text to fit within model limitations.

Let us consider a use case where we have a long passage of text, and we want to generate a concise summary of it using the OpenAI and LangChain libraries. We'll use a simple approach by splitting the text into smaller chunks and generating summaries for each chunk.

5.6.5 File name: app.py

```
import streamlit as st
from dotenv import load_dotenv
from utils import query_agent

load_dotenv()

st.title("Summarize data")
st.header("Please upload your text file :")

# Capture the CSV file
file = st.file_uploader("Upload Text file",type="txt")

#query = st.text_area("Enter your query")
button = st.button("Summarize and provide result")

if button:
    if file:

        if file.type=='text/plain':
```

```python
from io import StringIO
stringio=StringIO(file.getvalue().decode('utf-8'))
read_data=stringio.read()

# Get Response
answer =  query_agent(read_data)
st.write(answer)
```

5.6.6   File name: utils.py

```python
from langchain.llms import OpenAI
from langchain.text_splitter import CharacterTextSplitter
from langchain.docstore.document import Document
from langchain.chains.summarize import load_summarize_chain
import os

def query_agent(text):

    os.environ["OPENAI_API_KEY"] = "YOUR_API_KEY"

    llm = OpenAI(temperature=0.9)

    # Split text into chunks
    text_splitter = CharacterTextSplitter()
    texts = text_splitter.split_text(text)

    # Create the text into multiple documents
    docs = [Document(page_content=t) for t in texts]

    chain = load_summarize_chain(llm, chain_type="map_reduce")
    result=chain.run(docs)
    return(result
```

5.6.7   Arkansas.txt

Credits to hotels.com which explains the history of Arkansas as follows. Copy the below content into arkansas.txt file and save it. You will be uploading this file as an input source while running the program.

Arkansas borders the Mississippi River, with abundant parks, mountains, caves, and hot springs. You'll find no less than 50 state parks, 7 national parks, and 3 national forests – all of which are great for hiking, biking, kayaking, bathing, and other active adventures in nature. The Ozark–St. Francis National Forest attracts explorers looking to visit the Blanchard Springs Caverns, while the Hot Springs National Park has plenty of resorts with thermal baths containing naturally heated water.

A road trip through Arkansas often leads you to many towns and cities, most of which have family-friendly attractions, historical sites, fascinating museums, and diverse shopping opportunities. There are also unusual activities you won't find elsewhere in the USA, such as searching for real diamonds in the Crater of Diamonds State Park or exploring the ghost town of Rush in the Buffalo River National River Park.

Unknown Facts about Arkansas:

1. Did you know that Spanish explorer Hernando de Soto was the first European to reach Arkansas in 1541?

2. Fur trader Henri de Tonty, the Father of Arkansas, founded the first European Settlement on the Arkansas River.

3. Arkansas got its name from French settlers in the region. The word "Arkansas" is pronounced with a silent "s" at the end.

4. Interestingly, it is against state law to mispronounce the word "Arkansas" while in the state.

5. Arkansas is also the only state in North America where you can find a diamond field. The largest diamond ever discovered in North America was found in Crater of Diamonds State Park in 1924. At 40.23 carats, it was named "Uncle Sam." More than 33,100 diamonds have been found by park visitors since the Crater of Diamonds became an Arkansas state park in 1972.

6. The diamond mine is the only in the world that allows the public to keep what they find. Interestingly, a 13-year-old girl from Missouri found a 2.93-carat diamond in Crater of Diamonds State Park.

7. Did you know that diamonds are also Arkansas' state gem?

8. Rice production is a billion dollar industry in Arkansas. No doubt, Arkansas is the largest producer of rice among the 50 states.

9. *Rice production reportedly began in Arkansas in 1902 with one acre of rice grown in Lonoke County. However, some historical records suggest that rice was grown in some parts of Arkansas prior to the Civil War.*

10. *Milk was named the state beverage of Arkansas in 1985 to not only highlight the benefits of milk consumption, but also pay tribute to the importance of the bustling dairy industry in the state.*

5.6.8   Output generated.

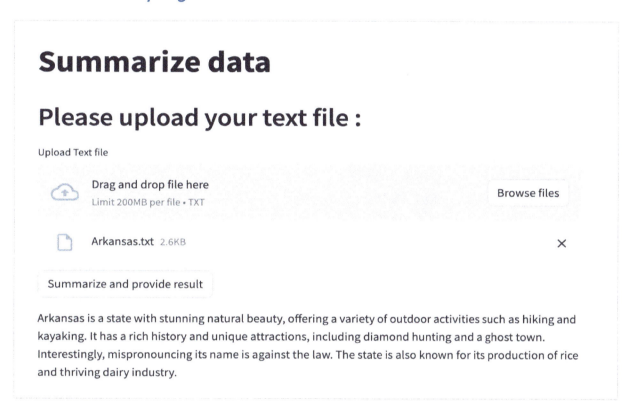

5.6.9   Conclusion

From the above example, we can conclude that the details of around 40 lines of Arkansas is summarized into 4-5 lines.

5.7   Mitigating Bias and Fairness Issues

Mitigating bias and addressing fairness issues in prompt engineering is a crucial aspect of responsible AI development. It involves designing prompts and using techniques that help reduce biases and promote fairness in the model's responses. Bias can be present in both the training data and the way prompts are formulated.

Let us consider a use case where we want to generate text related to gender-sensitive topics while minimizing gender bias. We'll use a simple example where the goal is to generate job descriptions that are neutral with respect to gender.

5.7.1   File name: MitigatingBiasAndFairness.py

```
from langchain.prompts import PromptTemplate
from langchain.llms import CTransformers

# Uses  https://huggingface.co/TheBloke/Llama-2-7B-Chat-GGML/tree/main

def mitigate_bias(question,max_tokens):
  prompt = f"Provide details for {question}."

  llm = CTransformers(model='models/llama-2-7b-chat.ggmlv3.q8_0.bin',
      model_type='llama',
      prompt=prompt,
      config={'max_new_tokens': max_tokens,
      'temperature': 0.01})

  response=llm(prompt.format(max_new_tokens=max_tokens))

  return response

max_tokens=100
question="Write a job description for a software engineer"
response = mitigate_bias(question,max_tokens)
```

print("Answer :", response)

5.7.2   *Output generated.*

Answer :
Job Title: Software Engineer

Job Summary:
We are seeking a highly skilled and motivated Software Engineer to join our team. The successful candidate will be responsible for designing, developing, testing, and maintaining software applications using various programming languages and technologies. The ideal candidate should have excellent problem-solving skills, be able to work independently or as part of a team, and have a strong commitment to deliver high-quality software products.

5.7.3   *Conclusion*

In this example, the prompt is designed to generate a job description for a software engineer. Here, the gender bias is avoided by default. However, it's important to note that gender bias may exist in the model's responses. To mitigate this bias, we can experiment with different prompts and carefully review and refine the generated text to ensure that it aligns with our goals of neutrality.

Copyrighted Material

6. Vector Store

The traditional RDBMS is used for organizing the data in the form of rows and columns as two-dimensional data. In the case of NO-SQL databases such as Hive, the data is stored in denormalized form to support the faster retrieval by addressing volume, veracity and variety. Also, we would have come across parquet-based data stored in Hive tables in columnar format which supports faster retrieval of sub-set of data to support the analytical applications. So, every data store has format for loading and indexing for retrieval of the data.

In the case of Vector store, its highly suitable for storing unstructured data such as texts, numbers, images, audio, video and others. It's highly used for storing vector embeddings, a numerical representation of data in high dimensional space. The dimensions can range from tens, thousands based on the granularity. Normally, we would have a seen data in 2-dimensional space RDBMS and in 3-dimensional space in graphs. It's difficult visualizing the view of vector embeddings in high dimensional space.

Vector DBs are used for similarity search and it supports multiple types of indexing and different retrieval algorithms depending on the DB used. It's important to understand that we can perform only similarity search which matches with the query in terms of semantics and not the exact search. When the Vector DB finds multiple documents based on the similarity search, it retrieves top matching documents from the existing embeddings. The query generation and request for retrieval are happening through raw data whereas the Vector DB converts the query data into embeddings i.e., in numerical format, tries to matches with the embeddings present in the DB, retrieves the matching embeddings and converts them into raw data format while displaying results.

We have to know few concepts about vectors such as magnitude, direction, Dot product, angle between the two vectors and Cosine similarity which are crucial to understand how Vector DB works actually.

6.1 What is a Vector?

Vector represent both magnitude and direction. The magnitude of a vector is represented by the vector size or length. The norm of a vector is the square root of the sum of square of each value and is represented as function(x) = sqrt(sum(x^2))

For example, let's assume that we have a vector a = (6,8). The magnitude of the vector is calculated as follows

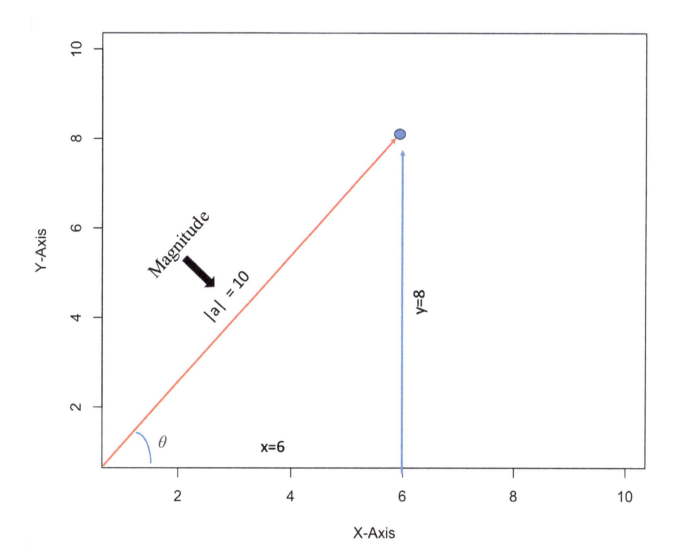

From the above picture you can understand that how a vector is represented on the plane. The θ represents the angle between the vector and x-axis. The magnitude is represented by the symbol |a| as below.

$|a| = Sqrt((6*6) + 8*8))$
$|a| = Sqrt(36+64)$
$|a| = 10$

The magnitude of the vector is 10.

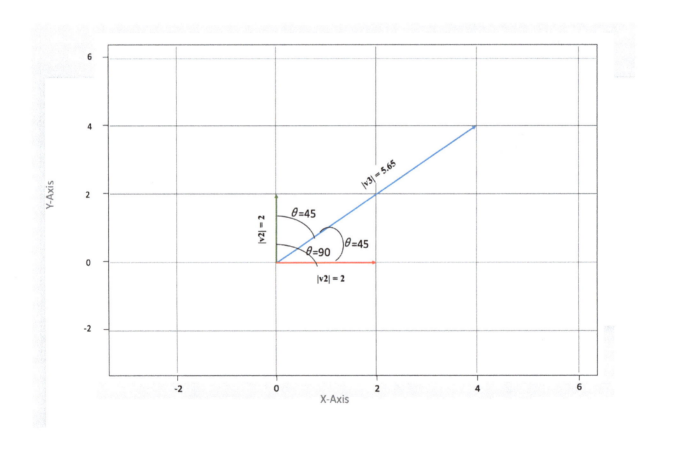

Now, let's consider 3 vectors v1, v2 and v3.

V1 = (2,0)
V2 = (0,2)
V3 = (4,4)

The magnitude is represented by the symbol |v1| as below.

|v1| = Sqrt((0*0) + 2*2))
|v1| = Sqrt(0+4)
|v1| = 2

The magnitude of |v2| is

|v2| = Sqrt((2*2) + 0*0))
|v2| = Sqrt(4+0)
|v2| = 2

The magnitude of |v3| is

|v2| = Sqrt((4*4) + 4*4))
|v2| = Sqrt(16+16)
|v2| = 5.65

6.2 Dot Product

The dot product is one of the most widely used vector operations for finding the similarity between the two vectors. The dot product is represented as Euclidean magnitude of two vectors and the cosine of the angle between them. The dot product takes two equal lengths of sequences of numbers and returns a number.

$$a.b = |a| * |b| * cos(\theta)$$

6.3 Cosine similarity

Based on the above formula, the cosine similarity can be calculated as follows by reversing the formula as follows:

$$cos(\theta) = a.b \,/\, (\,|a| * |b|\,)$$

This formula is used to find the similarities between two vectors. The result of the cosine similarity always ranges between -1 and 1. The Vector DBs apply this cosine similarity to search for the matching documents to perform similarity search.

6.4 Angle between two vectors

We can derive the angle between two vectors θ. using the dot product formula as follows

$$\theta = cos^{-1} [\, (\mathbf{a} \cdot \mathbf{b}) \,/\, (|\mathbf{a}|\, |\mathbf{b}|)\,]$$

Based on the above formulas, we understand the cosine similarity and the angle between two vectors which explains how far or how close they are against each other.

Cosine similarity is 1: When the value of cosine similarity is 1, the angle between the vectors becomes 0 degrees. This indicates that both vectors are the same which means that they point in the same direction.

Cosine similarity is 0: The angle between them is 90 degrees which means the two vectors are not related to each other.

Cosine similarity is -1: The angle between the 2 vector is 180 degrees which means that the two vectors are different and they point in opposite direction.

Let's consider the following 3-dimensional vectors. The vectors, X and Y have different values and are not the same. But let's find out geometrically, whether they are equal or not based on the cosine similarity formula

6.5 Example 1

Now, let's take a 3-dimensional vector for calculating the cosine similarity to find out to what extent they are similar.

$X = (1,2,3)$ and
$Y = (4,-5,6)$

The magnitude of X, |X| is

$|X| = Sqrt((1*1) + (2*2) + (3*3))$
$|X| = Sqrt(1+4+9)$
$|X| = Sqrt(14)$
$|X| = 3.74$

Same way, the magnitude of Y, |Y| is

$|Y| = Sqrt((4*4) + (-5*-5) + (6*6))$
$|Y| = Sqrt(16+25+36)$
$|Y| = Sqrt(77),$
$|Y| = 8.77$

The dot product of the 2 vectors is derived as follows:

$X.Y = (1 x4) + (2 * -5) + 3 * 6)$
$X.Y = 4 -10 + 18$
$X.Y = 12$

The dot product of the vectors X.Y is 12.

Now, we need to find the angle between the two vectors based on the dot product formula which is

$$X.Y = |X| * |Y| \ cos(\theta)$$

To find the angle between the two vectors, from the above formula, we can rewrite as follows:

$$Cosine\ similarity = cos(\theta) = X.Y\ /\ |X|\ *\ |Y|$$

$$cos(\theta) = 12\ /\ (3.74\ *\ 8.77)$$

$$cos(\theta) = 12\ /\ 32.79.\ = 0.36$$

$$Cosine\ similarity = cos(\theta) = 0.36$$

Conclusion: *For the above two vectors X and Y, the cosine similarity is 0.36 which is less than 1 which means that the 2 vectors are not same.*

The angle between the two vectors is calculated as follows:

> *θ, the angle between the two vectors is $= cos^{-1}\ (0.36)$ (inverse of cosine)*

$$\theta = 68.9\ °$$

The angle between the two vectors is 68.9 °

6.6 Example 2

This time, let's consider 2 vectors of same values for which we expect the cosine similarity value to become 1 in order to consider them as equal.

A = (1,2,3) and
B= (1,2,3)

The magnitude of A, |A| is

$|A| = Sqrt((1*1) + (2*2) + (3*3))$
$|A| = Sqrt(1+4+9)$
$|A| = Sqrt(14)$
$|A| = 3.74$

Same way, the magnitude of B, |B| is

$|B| = Sqrt((1*1) + (2*2) + (3*3))$
$|B| = Sqrt(1+4+9)$
$|B| = Sqrt(14)$
$|B| = 3.74$

The dot product of the 2 vectors is derived as follows:

$X.Y = (1 x1) + (2 * 2) + 3 * 3)$
$X.Y = 1 + 4 + 9$
$X.Y = 14$

To find the cosine similarity between 2 vectors,

$$cosine\ similarity = cos(\theta) = X.Y / |X| * |Y|$$

$$cos(\theta) = 14 / (13.98)$$

$$cos(\theta) = 14/(13.98)$$

$$cosine\ similarity = cos(\theta) = 1.00$$

From the above calculations, we have geometrically proved that the vectors A and B are the same.

From the angle between the vectors, we can understand the relationship between two vectors based on its direction and magnitude.

The reason why we have done the above calculation is that the cosine similarity is represented by the formula which is being used by Vector DB to find similarity between the encoded vector embeddings.

$$cos(\theta) = X.Y / |X| * |Y|$$

The cosine similarity also indicates the nearest neighbors. Let's consider how the nearest neighbor is interpreted for text embeddings using the example diagram below.

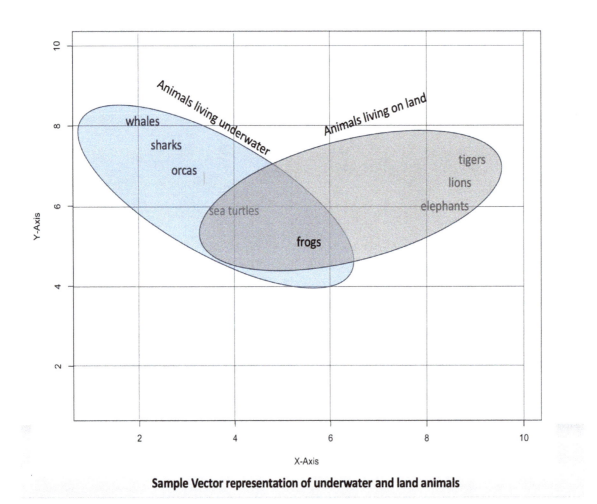

Sample Vector representation of underwater and land animals

The graph above shows how animals living underwater and on land are represented as vectors. In this picture, underwater animals include whales, sharks, orcas, sea turtles and frogs. Land animals include tigers, lions, elephants and frogs. Frogs are amphibians as they can live in both water and land.

Whales, sharks, and orcas are grouped closely together, while they are far from land animals like tigers, lions, and elephants.

If we observe the picture closely, sea turtles are a bit apart from other underwater animals and closer to land animals compared to other sea animals.

Sea turtles are positioned between the two groups because they briefly visit seashore to lay eggs but don't stay there for a long. That's why we've placed them between underwater and land animals but slightly closer to underwater animals than the land animals.

In the case of frogs, the frogs are placed almost in the middle of all underwater and land animals since the frogs are amphibians as they can live in both water and land.

What do we understand from the above vector representation is that the objects are placed in vector coordinates along with the values that representants the relative similarities of neighboring objects called vector embeddings. These vector embeddings are created based on cosine similarity or nearest neighbor algorithms.

Now, if you query the vector DB to list out top-3 animals, it will return tigers, lions and elephants. Now, you can notice that frogs and turtles are not given priority within the top-3 list. The underwater animals are ignored by default from the top-3 list.

When you reformat the query to display top-4 animals list from the vector db, it will list out tigers, lions, elephants and frogs.

When you reformat the query to display top-5 animals list from the vector db, it will list out tigers, lions, elephants, frogs and sea turtles. But, the underwater animals are ignored.

What we understand from the above query results is that the elements are placed in the vector db based on the order, category and with its relative distance with each neighbor. Also, we have to notice that the vector representation for each neighboring element is calculated in run time based on each query sent. This model of vector representation helps to perform the similarity search. Because, when you want to list out all underwater elements, naturally tigers, lions and elephants will be ignored.

Having understood, how vector DB is used for finding the similarity encoded vectors, let's get into the sample implementation strategies using Python.

 Copyrighted Material

6.7 Steps for loading Data into Vector DB

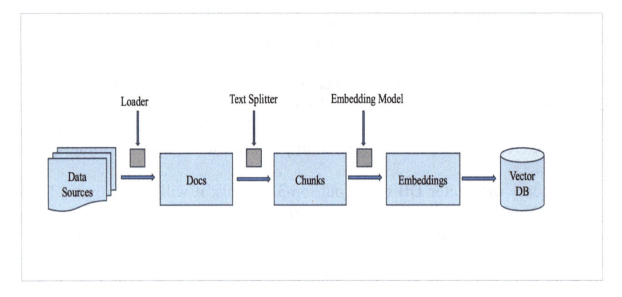

Retrieval augmented generation (RAG)

6.7.1.1 Documents

Vector DB can process various types of documents such as text, images, videos, audio, PDF files, and more. These documents are stored in Vector DB as encoded vector embeddings. Let's explore how this process works in the following steps.

6.7.1.2 Chunks

The documents that feed in into the AI model is divided into multiple chunks based on the text splitter. While splitting the document into multiple chunks, we can overlap fixed number of number of characters between the adjacent chunks to provide the continuity. The number of characters to overlap can be set through the parameter while splitting the documents.

6.7.1.3 *Vector Embeddings*

Vector embeddings are the numerical representation of data stored in the vector store. The objects such as text data, image, audio, video can be converted into numerical vectors using embedding model and stored in the vector store for performing similarity search, grouping and categorization of data.

For example, once you save your text data into Vector DB as vectors, let's assume that you are performing similarity search by sending a query, the query passed is again converted into vector embeddings and it performs dot product-based cosine similarity search on the vector DB to retrieve the results. For performing search and retrieval of data, the processing happens through vector embeddings format. When the numerical vector matching our query is identified, its converted back to raw format and returned to the users.

6.7.1.4 *Vector DB*

The primary advantage of a vector DB is its storage in a high-dimensional space, making it scalable and efficient in search operations. This results in increased performance. Additionally, it can store various types of unstructured data such as text, images, audio, and video.

Vector DB supports several operations including adding documents, querying documents, updating, deleting, and upserting. The difference between updating and upserting lies in their behavior:

- When you use the update command, if the document ID exists, it gets updated. However, if the document ID is not found, an error is thrown stating "document ID does not exist."

- In the case of upsert, the document is updated if it already exists. If it doesn't exist, the document is inserted. This process is called upsert.

Next, we shall discuss how Python programming can be used for similarity search against vector db.

6.8 Execution using ChromaDB

Now, let's explore how to run a query using a vector DB. In this scenario, we'll focus on ChromaDB since it's an open-source tool. Another popular Vector DB called Pinecone, on the other hand, requires a subscription charge. Since, our goal is to understand the vector db programming, we will be using Chroma DB to help our readers to understand the concepts. As part of the example, we will load a text file into Chroma DB and try to perform similarity search using Python programming.

6.8.1.1 File name: requirements.txt

openai
langchain
chromadb
sentence_transformers

Please install the APIs first by running the command given below

pip install -r requirements.txt

6.8.1.2 File name: DataLoadIntoChromaDB.py

In the following sample Python code, we read text data from a file and split it into multiple chunks of size 10 with no overlapping. Once we have the chunks, we use the pre-trained model all-MiniLM-L6-v2 from HuggingFace for semantic search to create the vector embeddings, which are then loaded into ChromaDB.

Next, we develop a retriever with the syntax search_kwargs={"k": 3}, indicating that we want to send the top 3 matching vectors to the prompt.

When we send a query such as *"What animals are present?"*, *it* is converted into vector embeddings. A similarity search is then executed between the query embeddings and the loaded embeddings in the vector DB, identifying and retrieving the top 3 matching animals from the vector DB.

Please review the output displayed under the headers "Printing results for animals" and "Printing results for flowers."

We have also provided sample outputs generated during the execution of the program to explain how the data is stored in the vector DB with metadata labels indicating the source file name.

6.8.1.3   *File name: GetMeAnswersFromDB.py*

```
from langchain.document_loaders import TextLoader
from langchain.text_splitter import CharacterTextSplitter
from langchain.embeddings import OpenAIEmbeddings
from langchain.vectorstores import Chroma
from langchain.chains import RetrievalQA
from langchain.embeddings.sentence_transformer import
SentenceTransformerEmbeddings


# Load the input file
inputFile = TextLoader('Sample.txt')
data = inputFile.load()

# Split the text into multiple chunks of size 10 with overlapping of 0 characters
text_splitter = CharacterTextSplitter (chunk_size=10,chunk_overlap=0)
chunks= text_splitter.split_documents(data)

print("Printing Chunks")
print("--------------")
print(chunks)
print("")
```

Copyrighted Material

```
print("")
embeddings = SentenceTransformerEmbeddings(model_name="all-MiniLM-L6-v2")

db = Chroma.from_documents(chunks, embeddings)
db._collection.get(include=['embeddings'])
retriever = db.as_retriever(search_kwargs={"k": 3})


print("printing retriever")
print("-------------------")
print(retriever)
print("")
print("")


docs = retriever.get_relevant_documents("What animals are present?")
print("Printing Results now for list of animals")
print("=======================================")
print(docs)
print("")
print("")
docs = retriever.get_relevant_documents("What flowers are present?")
print("Printing Results now for list of flowers")
print("=======================================")
print(docs)
```

6.8.1.4 *Sample.txt*

Please create this file with one line space in-between each line.

Tiger

Lion

Elephant

Jasmine

Rose

Lavender

Apple

6.8.1.5 *Output generated by the model*

$ python GetMeAnswers.py
Printing Chunks

[Document(page_content='Tiger', metadata={'source': 'Sample.txt'}),
Document(page_content='Lion', metadata={'source': 'Sample.txt'}),
Document(page_content='Elephant', metadata={'source': 'Sample.txt'}),
Document(page_content='Jasmine', metadata={'source': 'Sample.txt'}),
Document(page_content='Rose', metadata={'source': 'Sample.txt'}),
Document(page_content='Lavender', metadata={'source': 'Sample.txt'}),
Document(page_content='Apple', metadata={'source': 'Sample.txt'})]

/opt/homebrew/anaconda3/lib/python3.11/site-packages/torch/_utils.py:831:
UserWarning: TypedStorage is deprecated. It will be removed in the future and
UntypedStorage will be the only storage class. This should only matter to you if you
are using storages directly. To access UntypedStorage directly, use
tensor.untyped_storage() instead of tensor.storage()
  return self.fget.__get__(instance, owner)()
printing retriever
----

tags=['Chroma', 'HuggingFaceEmbeddings']
vectorstore=<langchain_community.vectorstores.chroma.Chroma object at
0x2b708ead0> search_kwargs={'k': 3}

Printing Results now for list of animals
===

[Document(page_content='Elephant', metadata={'source': 'Sample.txt'}),
Document(page_content='Lion', metadata={'source': 'Sample.txt'}),
Document(page_content='Tiger', metadata={'source': 'Sample.txt'})]

Printing Results now for list of flowers
===
[Document(page_content='Lavender', metadata={'source': 'Sample.txt'}),
Document(page_content='Rose', metadata={'source': 'Sample.txt'}),
Document(page_content='Jasmine', metadata={'source': 'Sample.txt'})]

6.8.1.6   *File name: QAFromChromaDB*

In this program, we input a text file which is divided into multiple chunks of 100 characters length with overlap values of 0. You can notice that the document is split into 35 chunks for loading into ChromaDB and next we will send a question to perform similarity search and retrieval.

For this program, we are looking for a top first answer for the given query based on the retrieval criteria given as "search_kwargs={"k": 1})". As expected, the model returns the best matching answer from the vector DB.

from langchain.document_loaders import TextLoader
from langchain.text_splitter import RecursiveCharacterTextSplitter
from langchain.vectorstores import Chroma
from langchain.embeddings.sentence_transformer import
SentenceTransformerEmbeddings
from langchain.document_loaders import TextLoader

 # Load the Arkansas.txt file
 # Load the input file
inputFile = TextLoader('Arkansas.txt')
documents = inputFile.load()

```
# Print the number of documents loaded
print(len(documents))
1

# Split text into chunks though the size is given as 100, the
text_splitter = RecursiveCharacterTextSplitter(
    chunk_size = 100,
    chunk_overlap  = 0,
    length_function = len,
)

# the data  is split into  multiple documents of 100 character length
texts= text_splitter.split_documents(documents)


# print how many chunks are created using text splitter
# Its printing below that 35 documents have been created from the text file
len(texts)

35
```

The above number 35 indicates that the document is divided into 35 chunks of 100 characters. Each chunk is again called as a document.

```
#prints the chunks created with source id. Here the source id is nothing but the
document name. This helps to understand how the documents are split into 35 chunks.
Also, you can notice that the document name appears for the source in the metadata.
print(texts)
```

The 35 documents created are listed below for your understanding to explain how the documents are organized. You can also notice that metadata is also created to indicate from which file the documents are sourced.

```
[Document(page_content='Arkansas borders the Mississippi River, with abundant
parks, mountains, caves, and hot springs.', metadata={'source': 'Arkansas.txt'}),
```

Document(page_content='You'll find no less than 50 state parks, 7 national parks, and 3 national forests – all of which', metadata={'source': 'Arkansas.txt'}), Document(page_content='are great for hiking, hiking, kayaking, bathing, and other active adventures in nature. The', metadata={'source': 'Arkansas.txt'}), Document(page_content='Ozark–St. Francis National Forest attracts explorers looking to visit the Blanchard Springs', metadata={'source': 'Arkansas.txt'}), Document(page_content='Caverns, while the Hot Springs National Park has plenty of resorts with thermal baths containing', metadata={'source': 'Arkansas.txt'}), Document(page_content='naturally heated water.', metadata={'source': 'Arkansas.txt'}), Document(page_content='A road trip through Arkansas often leads you to many towns and cities, most of which have', metadata={'source': 'Arkansas.txt'}), Document(page_content='family-friendly attractions, historical sites, fascinating museums, and diverse shopping', metadata={'source': 'Arkansas.txt'}), Document(page_content='opportunities. There are also unusual activities you won't find elsewhere in the USA, such as', metadata={'source': 'Arkansas.txt'}), Document(page_content='searching for real diamonds in the Crater of Diamonds State Park or exploring the ghost town of', metadata={'source': 'Arkansas.txt'}), Document(page_content='Rush in the Buffalo River National River Park.', metadata={'source': 'Arkansas.txt'}), Document(page_content='Unknown Facts about Arkansas:', metadata={'source': 'Arkansas.txt'}), Document(page_content='1. Did you know that Spanish explorer Hernando de Soto was the first European to reach Arkansas in', metadata={'source': 'Arkansas.txt'}), Document(page_content='1541?', metadata={'source': 'Arkansas.txt'}), Document(page_content='2. Fur trader Henri de Tonty, the Father of Arkansas, founded the first European Settlement on the', metadata={'source': 'Arkansas.txt'}), Document(page_content='Arkansas River.', metadata={'source': 'Arkansas.txt'}), Document(page_content='3. Arkansas got its name from French settlers in the region. The word "Arkansas" is pronounced with', metadata={'source': 'Arkansas.txt'}), Document(page_content='a silent "s" at the end.', metadata={'source': 'Arkansas.txt'}), Document(page_content='4. Interestingly, it is against state law to mispronounce the word "Arkansas" while in the state.', metadata={'source': 'Arkansas.txt'}), Document(page_content='5. Arkansas is also the only state in North America where you can find a diamond field. The largest', metadata={'source': 'Arkansas.txt'}), Document(page_content='diamond ever discovered in North America was found in Crater of Diamonds State Park in 1924. At', metadata={'source': 'Arkansas.txt'}), Document(page_content='40.23 carats, it was named "Uncle Sam." More than 33,100 diamonds have been found by park visitors', metadata={'source': 'Arkansas.txt'}), Document(page_content='since the Crater of Diamonds became an Arkansas state park in 1972.', metadata={'source': 'Arkansas.txt'}), Document(page_content='6. The diamond mine is the only in the

Copyrighted Material

world that allows the public to keep what they find.', metadata={'source': 'Arkansas.txt'}), Document(page_content='Interestingly, a 13-year-old girl from Missouri found a 2.93-carat diamond in Crater of Diamonds', metadata={'source': 'Arkansas.txt'}), Document(page_content='State Park.', metadata={'source': 'Arkansas.txt'}), Document(page_content='7. Did you know that diamonds are also Arkansas' state gem?', metadata={'source': 'Arkansas.txt'}), Document(page_content='8. Rice production is a billion dollar industry in Arkansas. No doubt, Arkansas is the largest', metadata={'source': 'Arkansas.txt'}), Document(page_content='producer of rice among the 50 states.', metadata={'source': 'Arkansas.txt'}), Document(page_content='9. Rice production reportedly began in Arkansas in 1902 with one acre of rice grown in Lonoke', metadata={'source': 'Arkansas.txt'}), Document(page_content='County. However, some historical records suggest that rice was grown in some parts of Arkansas', metadata={'source': 'Arkansas.txt'}), Document(page_content='prior to the Civil War.', metadata={'source': 'Arkansas.txt'}), Document(page_content='10. Milk was named the state beverage of Arkansas in 1985 to not only highlight the benefits of', metadata={'source': 'Arkansas.txt'}), Document(page_content='milk consumption, but also pay tribute to the importance of the bustling dairy industry in the', metadata={'source': 'Arkansas.txt'}), Document(page_content='state.', metadata={'source': 'Arkansas.txt'})]

Now, let's create an embedding model by referring to the HuggingFace Sentence Transformer Embeddings model all-MiniLM0L6-v2. We are using this model to create vector embeddings in order to store them into Vector DB.

 # Use the pre-trained model to create the embeddings.
 # embedding contains encoded values for each chunks created
embeddings = SentenceTransformerEmbeddings(model_name="all-MiniLM-L6-v2")

From the below statement, we convert the 35 documents into the vector embeddings in the numerical form.

 # store the embeddings as vector store in ChromaDB
db = Chroma.from_documents(texts, embeddings)

 Copyrighted Material

Now, let's try to retrieve the vector embeddings to see the format of the vector embeddings. The below command retrieves the vector embeddings from the DB.

 # now, we can see the embeddings in numeric format stored in vector db
db.collection.get(include=['embeddings'])

Vector embeddings are displayed below:

```
{'ids': ['110b26ee-b5ab-11ee-b888-aa77c063adea',
  '110b273e-b5ab-11ee-b888-aa77c063adea',
  '110b2752-b5ab-11ee-b888-aa77c063adea',
  '110b275c-b5ab-11ee-b888-aa77c063adea',
  '110b2770-b5ab-11ee-b888-aa77c063adea',
  '110b277a-b5ab-11ee-b888-aa77c063adea',
  '110b278e-b5ab-11ee-b888-aa77c063adea',
  '110b27ac-b5ab-11ee-b888-aa77c063adea',
  '110b27b6-b5ab-11ee-b888-aa77c063adea',
  '110b27ca-b5ab-11ee-b888-aa77c063adea',
  '110b27d4-b5ab-11ee-b888-aa77c063adea',
  '110b27e8-b5ab-11ee-b888-aa77c063adea',
  '110b27f2-b5ab-11ee-b888-aa77c063adea',
  '110b27fc-b5ab-11ee-b888-aa77c063adea',
  '110b2810-b5ab-11ee-b888-aa77c063adea',
  '110b281a-b5ab-11ee-b888-aa77c063adea',
  '110b2824-b5ab-11ee-b888-aa77c063adea',
  '110b2838-b5ab-11ee-b888-aa77c063adea',
  '110b2842-b5ab-11ee-b888-aa77c063adea',
  '110b284c-b5ab-11ee-b888-aa77c063adea',
  '110b2856-b5ab-11ee-b888-aa77c063adea',
  '110b286a-b5ab-11ee-b888-aa77c063adea',
  '110b2874-b5ab-11ee-b888-aa77c063adea',
  '110b287e-b5ab-11ee-b888-aa77c063adea',
  '110b2888-b5ab-11ee-b888-aa77c063adea',
...
  0.03613627329468727]],
'metadatas': None,
'documents': None,
'uris': None,
```

'data': None}
Output is truncated. View as a <u>scrollable element</u> or open in a <u>text editor</u>. Adjust cell output <u>settings</u>...

Now, we want to decide how many answers are to be retrieved from the vector DB for the question sent to the DB. In this case, we want to retrieve the topmost answer by specifying "k": 1.

 # we want to retrieve only one matching document from the vector DB for the query raised.
 # k=1 means, it retrieves only one top matching document which is closer to the question.
retriever = db.as_retriever(search_kwargs={"k": 1})

Now, the question is sent to the vector DB with the value

"Who was the first European to reach Arkansas?"

Internally, the text of the question is converted into vector embeddings in numerical form since vector DB can perform numerical comparisons. The DB then performs cosine similarity function to find the embeddings that match the most, retrieves the embeddings, and displays them in the document format, which represents the topmost matching document from the list of 35 available documents.

question="Who was the first European to reach Arkansas?"
result = retriever.get_relevant_documents(question)

The result of the matching document is displayed below:

print(result)
[Document(page_content='1. Did you know that Spanish explorer Hernando de Soto was the first European to reach Arkansas in', metadata={'source': 'Arkansas.txt'})]

7.   HuggingFace Application release strategy

HuggingFace provides public spaces for development and deployment of LLM applications through endpoints which empowers developers to deploy LLM application in an easiest and quickest way without having the need to manage the infrastructure by offering the environment for development, testing, deployment and sharing of applications with the data science community.

As part of the application release requirement, we are going to use the HuggingFace environment for deploying our model. To deploy an application in the HuggingFace environment, you have to create an account and generate an HuggingFace key, as shown in the snapshot below.

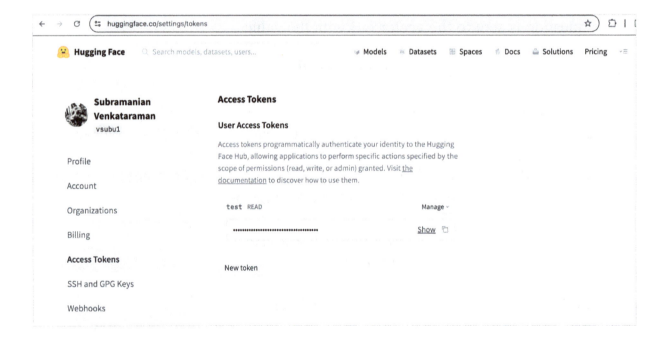

Copyrighted Material

7.1   Deployment with HuggingFace

HuggingFace provides an interface for deploying files and running applications in either private or public mode. In private mode, only the developer will have access to the application and its codes, whereas in public mode, the entire user community will have access to the application and source codes. It's important to decide how you want to deploy your application.

The HuggingFace environment offers options to create files, set up API keys, and run installations using a requirements.txt file. Using this approach, the application can be set up in the target environment.

As an example, let's deploy the codes generated for TextGeneration.py, which will be deployed in HuggingFace as the "TellMeAStory" application. To deploy, we need to split the files into app.py and utils.py.

The app.py file will read the API keys and prompt the user for inputs regarding the Age group (Kids, Teens, or Adult) and the story type (Suspense, Thrillers, Adventure, Fantasy, Historical, Fiction, Horror, or Mystery). Once the inputs are received, the user will press the 'Generate' button. The application will respond with 'Processing...' and start generating the story.

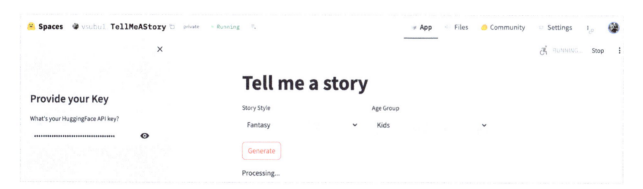

Once the story is printed, the UI will be as follows:

Here are the contents of all files that we deploy into HuggingFace environment as part this process.

Copyrighted Material

7.1.1   File name: app.py

```
import streamlit as st
from langchain.prompts import PromptTemplate
from langchain.llms import CTransformers
from utils import *

#Uses https://huggingface.co/TheBloke/Llama-2-7B-Chat-GGML/tree/main
# Creating Session State Variable
if 'HuggingFace_API_Key' not in st.session_state:
    st.session_state['HuggingFace_API_Key'] =''

st.title("Tell me a story")

# Sidebar to capture the API keys
st.sidebar.title("Provide your Key")
st.session_state['HuggingFace_API_Key']= st.sidebar.text_input("What's your
HuggingFace API key?",type="password")

#Creating columns for the UI - To receive inputs from user
col1, col2, col3 = st.columns([10, 10, 5])
with col1:
    story_style = st.selectbox('Story Style',
                    ('Suspense', 'Thrillers', 'Adventure', 'Fantasy', 'Historical',
'Fiction', 'Horror', 'Mystery'),
                        index=0)
with col2:
    age_group = st.selectbox('Age Group',
                    ('Kids', 'Teenagers', 'Adult'),
                        index=0)
submit = st.button("Generate")
st.write("Processing...")
```

```python
#When 'Generate' button is clicked, execute the below code
if submit:
    st.write(getResponse(story_style,age_group))
```

7.1.2   File name: utils.py

```python
from langchain.prompts import PromptTemplate
from langchain.llms import CTransformers
import streamlit as st

#https://huggingface.co/TheBloke/Llama-2-7B-Chat-GGML/tree/main
#Function to get the response back
def getResponse(story_style, age_group):

    #Proceed only if API keys are provided
    if st.session_state['HuggingFace_API_Key'] !="" :
        llm = CTransformers(model="TheBloke/Llama-2-7B-Chat-GGML",
                model_type='llama',
                config={'max_new_tokens': 256,
                    'temperature': 0.01})


        #Template for building the PROMPT
        template = """
        Write a moral story based on the {story_style} for the {age_group} in 50 lines
        \n\nStory Text :
        """
        #Creating the final PROMPT
        prompt = PromptTemplate(
        input_variables=["story_style","age_group"],
        template=template,)

        #Generating the response using LLM
        response=llm(prompt.format(story_style=story_style,age_group=age_group))

        return (response)
    else:
        st.sidebar.error(" Please provide the API keys.....")
```

7.1.3   *File name: requirements.txt*

openai
langchain
huggingface-hub
streamlit
transformers
utils
ctransformers

7.1.4   *Create new Space*

In order to deploy the files, go to the URL **https://huggingface.co/username**
Click on your profile icon and select ''New Space' menu. Now, Huggingface opens
up the page as follows:

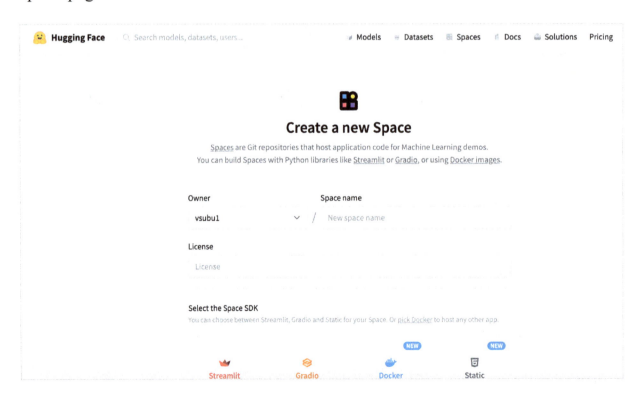

Creating a new space involves creating an application name for deploying your files. Your application will be visible in private or public mode based on the options chosen with this space name. You have to enter your new application name and select the environment you want to use for running the job. In our case, we are using Streamlit for running the application name through which the UI features are designed. Then choose the space/hardware. In this case, we have chosen the Free tier where the system allocates limited resources and memory for running the jobs, which is currently good enough for running this job.

7.1.5   Deployment of files

Next, you have to deploy the files that we have given above with the names app.py, utils.py and requirements.txt into the Huggingface. For this, please go to the URL **https://huggingface.co/spaces/username/TellMeAStory** and click on 'Files' menu.

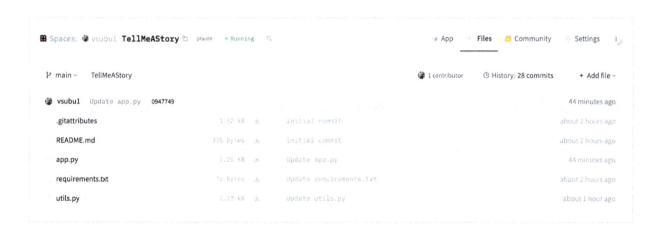

Here, please click on '+ Add file' and copy & paste your file contents into the corresponding file names as given above.

7.1.6   Building the Application

Once the files are transferred, you are good to start the application. To start the application, please click on the 'App' menu.

Then HuggingFace starts building your project. Please refer to the snapshot given below to indicate how HuggingFace starts building the application.

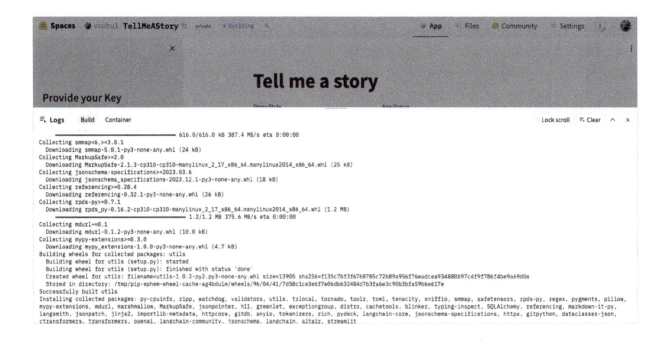

7.1.7 *Running the application*

Once the build is completed, provide the inputs for the HuggingFace API Key. Select the 'Story Style' and 'Age Group' from the drop-downs and click on the 'Generate' button. Then, the application starts running as shown below in the snapshot.

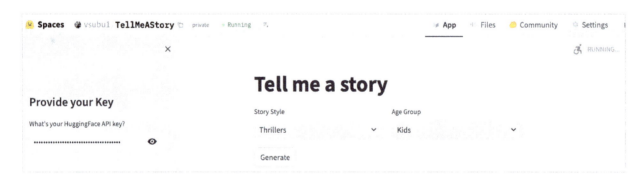

7.1.7.1 *Output generated by the model*

Once the processing is completed, the story is generated as shown below in the snapshot, which may not be the same every time as the model re-generates a new story each time. Please note that due to the maximum number of tokens defined, the story is truncated after the limit is reached. Please set the maximum limit as needed in your application.

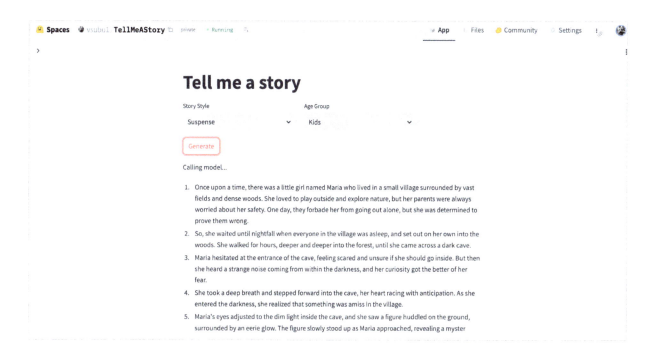

Now, your application, 'TellMeAStory,' is available for execution in the form of an 'App' as shown below. You can click on the app and start the execution of the application.

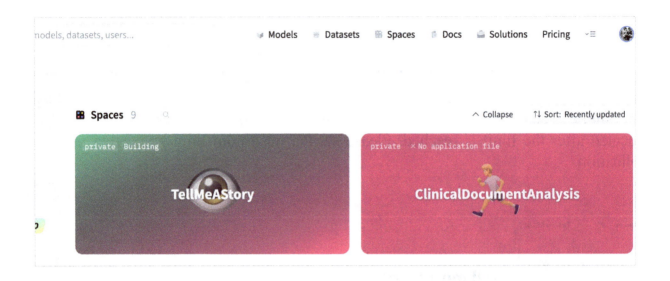

7.2 Deployment of applications

Deploying prompt-engineered models involves integrating our language model with an application or service, making it accessible to end-users. The deployment process may vary depending on the specific use case, the chosen model, and the technology stack we are working with.

- Models can be deployed in public using solutions offered by open-source tools like HuggingFace
- Using Retrieval Augmented Generation (RAG) , using Vector DBs such as
  - Pinecone, a proprietary cloud-based vector database offers optimized storage and querying capabilities for embeddings.
  - ChromaDB, an open-source DB primarily designed for LLMs, Pgvector, a vector DB highly suitable for similarity search requirements and is an extension of PostgreSQL DB.

Copyrighted Material

8. Sample Use Cases

In this chapter we will discuss few uses for explaining how to use Prompt engineering by defining prompts in a structured way to interact with LLMs by sending the questions and receiving the appropriate answers. These uses cases are demonstrated using Open AI's pre-trained models and HuggingFace models.

8.1 Question Answering: Answering Questions from a Passage

8.1.1 Filename: QuestionAnsweringFromPassage.py

In this example we are sending a prompt to the Open AI model to generate a response to the question based on the given passage hardcoded in the program. As part of this program, we preset the prompt to display an answer for the specific question or the model displays "No specific topic found" message if no answer is found.

```
import openai
# Replace " YOUR_OPENAI_API_KEY" with your actual OpenAI API key for this
code to work.

openai.api_key = "YOUR_OPENAI_API_KEY"
GPT_MODEL = "gpt-3.5-turbo"

document_list = """ Speech-to-Text Conversion: The first step in voice recognition is
converting spoken words into text. This process, known as speech-to-text or automatic
speech recognition (ASR), involves analyzing audio signals and transcribing them into
written form.
2. Natural Language Understanding (NLU): Once the spoken words are converted to
text, NLP techniques are applied to understand the meaning and intent behind the
words.
3. Intent Recognition: Identifying the user's intent based on the voice command is a
crucial step. Virtual assistants use NLP models to recognize the specific action or task
the user is requesting.
4. Response Generation: After understanding the user's intent, the virtual assistant
generates an appropriate response. This can involve looking up information,
performing actions, or providing relevant details.
5. Voice Synthesis (Text-to-Speech): In cases where the virtual assistant needs to
respond vocally, the system uses text-to-speech (TTS) technology to convert the
written response into spoken words.
"""

query = f"""Use the given passage from document_list to answer the question. If you
don't find any answer, write "No specific topic found."

Article:
\"\"\"
{document_list}
\"\"\"

Question: Explain NLU"""
```

Copyrighted Material

```
response = openai.chat.completions.create(
    messages=[
        {'role': 'system', 'content': 'You answer questions from the given passage.'},
        {'role': 'user', 'content': query},
    ],
    model=GPT_MODEL,
    temperature=0,
)
print(response.choices[0].message.content)
```

8.1.2   Output generated the model

```
$ python -m streamlit run QuestionAnsw
eringFromPassage.py

  You can now view your Streamlit app in your browser.

  Local URL: http://localhost:8501

NLU stands for Natural Language Understanding. It is a process that is applied after converting spoken words i
nto text through speech-to-text conversion. NLU techniques are used to understand the meaning and intent behin
d the words. In the context of voice recognition, NLU helps virtual assistants or systems to comprehend and in
terpret the user's commands or queries accurately. It involves analyzing the text and extracting relevant info
rmation to determine the user's intention or desired action. NLU plays a crucial role in enabling virtual assi
stants to provide appropriate and relevant responses to user queries or commands.
```

In this example, the prompt and the input passage are hardcoded., In the upcoming examples, we will see how to generalize the prompts and how to use data from various sources to get answers for our questions.

8.2 Sentiment Analysis

Copyrighted Material

In this example, we will discuss how LLM is applied to analyze the sentiment for a given statement passed through the prompt.

The primary goal of this example is to understand:

- The sentiment expressed in these texts.
- How LLM techniques can help us to automate the process of sentiment analysis

8.2.1   *File name: SentimentAnalysis.py*

As an example, let's create a simplified example using the Llama-2 - HuggingFace API for sentiment analysis and print the results.

```
from langchain.prompts import PromptTemplate
from langchain.llms import CTransformers

# Uses https://huggingface.co/TheBloke/Llama-2-7B-Chat-GGML/tree/main

#Function to generate the response
def getLLMResponse(statement):
    llm = CTransformers(model='models/llama-2-7b-chat.ggmlv3.q8_0.bin',
            model_type='llama',
            config={'max_new_tokens': 256,
                'temperature': 0.3})


    #Template for PROMPT
    template = """
    What is the sentiment of the {statement}.
    \n\nStatement:

    """

    #building the PROMPT
```

```
prompt = PromptTemplate(
input_variables=["statement"],
template=template)

#GGetting the response from LLM
response=llm(prompt.format(statement=statement))

return response

# sample texts for  doing sentiment analysis
text_list = [
    "The Ozark park is beautiful to watch during fall season.",
    "The tea is not hot",
]

# Process each statement from the text_list
i=1
for  statement in text_list:
    print("\n\n")
    print(f"{i}. Content: {statement}")
    print(f" Sentiment: {getLLMResponse(statement)}")
    i=i+1
```

This example uses the Llama-2 library using the llama-2-7b-chat.ggmlv3.q8_0.bin model   from Huggingface, which provides a simple API for common NLP tasks. Sentiment analysis is performed on a list of sample texts. The sentiments are categorized in to positive or negative and printed in the console.

8.2.1.1   *Output generated the model*

The output generated sentiment as "Negative" and "Positive" for the content we added below.

```
                                                      $ python SocialMediaMonitoring.py

1. Content: The Ozark park is beautiful to watch during fall season.
   Sentiment: "The Ozark park is beautiful to watch during fall season."

Sentiment Analysis:
Positive



2. Content: The tea is not hot
   Sentiment:  The tea is not hot.

Sentiment:
Negative
```

8.3 Named Entities

Entity Recognition, also known as Named Entity Recognition (NER), is the main task in Natural Language Processing (NLP) that involves identifying and classifying entities within unstructured text data. Example for named entities are names of people, locations, organizations, dates, and other specific categories. In this program, we are using LLAM2 model for extracting entities from the paragraph.

Example Code in Python:

Let us create a simplified example with a pre-trained model from HuggingFace, llama-2-7b-chat.ggmlv3.q8_0.bin API. In the program, we have configured the prompt with an instruction "Extract named entities" to extract the named entities alone from the given input paragraph. The model is able to identify the named entities and list them in the UI, which you can see in the output.

8.3.1 Input Text

The input text used for the execution of the code is given below:

The COO of the XYZ limited, TX, USA is the head of the operations who handles the business development across USA, UK and India. The COO is assisted by CEO who oversees the normal day-today operations of the organization. The CEO is assisted by CTO, CHRO and CQO who handles the Technology division, Human Resources Division and Quality Process division. The company has at next level supported by Project Managers, Team Leads who handles around 500 employees. The turnover of the company in 2021-2023 was 140 million US dollars. for 2022-2023, the company is expecting to reach the turnover of around 200 million dollars.

8.3.2   *File name: Ner.py*

```
import streamlit as st
from langchain.prompts import PromptTemplate
from langchain.llms import CTransformers

# Uses https://huggingface.co/TheBloke/Llama-2-7B-Chat-GGML/tree/main

#Function to get the response back
def getLLMResponse(text):

    llm = CTransformers(model='models/llama-2-7b-chat.ggmlv3.q8_0.bin',
            model_type='llama',
            config={'max_new_tokens': 256,
                'temperature': 0.01})



    #Template for building the PROMPT
    template = """
    Extract the named entities from the  {text}.
    """

    #Creating the final PROMPT
    prompt = PromptTemplate(
    input_variables=["text"],
    template=template)

    #Generating the response using LLM
```

```
response=llm(prompt.format(text=text))
print(response)

return response
```

```
st.markdown("<h1 style='text-align: center;'>Extract named entities </h1>",
unsafe_allow_html=True)
```

```
#Creating columns for the UI - To receive inputs from user
statement = st.text_area('Enter your Statements', height=10)
```

```
submit = st.button("Generate")
```

```
#When 'Generate' button is clicked, execute the below code
if submit:
    st.write(getLLMResponse(statement))
```

8.3.3   Output generated by the model

Extract named entities

Enter your Statements
was 140 million US dollars. for 2022-2023, the company is expecting to reach the turnover of around 200
million dollars.

Generate

The named entities are: - XYZ limited - TX, USA - CEO - CTO - CHRO - CQO - Project Managers - Team Leads

The named entities in the text are:

1. XYZ limited
2. TX, USA
3. CEO
4. CTO
5. CHRO
6. CQO
7. Project Managers
8. Team Leads

8.4 Clinical document analysis

LLMs are being used in healthcare for extracting details from clinical documents. The clinical documents are mostly in image, PDF, or text files.

In this example, we will use OpenAI LLM to analyze and extract information from PDF documents by assuming that PDF files contain patient information. The extracted information can be downloaded into a CSV file in a structured format.

8.4.1 File name: app.py

```python
import streamlit as st
from dotenv import load_dotenv
from utils import *
from  utils import create_docs

def main():
    load_dotenv()
    st.set_page_config(page_title="Clinical Document Extraction")
    st.title("Extract Clinical Documents")
    st.subheader("Extracting clinical documents")

    # Upload your clinical records in pdf format
    pdf = st.file_uploader("Upload the clinical documents here in PDF format",
type=["pdf"],accept_multiple_files=True)

    submit=st.button("Extract Data")

    if submit:
        with st.spinner('Wait for it...'):
            df=create_docs(pdf)
            st.write(df.head())

            data_as_csv= df.to_csv(index=False).encode("utf-8")
            st.download_button(
                "Download data as CSV",
```

```python
            data_as_csv,
            "benchmark-tools.csv",
            "text/csv",
            key="download-tools-csv",
        )

#main function is called
if __name__ == '__main__':
    main()
```

8.4.2   *File name: utils.py*

```python
from langchain.llms import OpenAI
from pypdf import PdfReader
from langchain.llms.openai import OpenAI
import pandas as pd
import re
from langchain.prompts import PromptTemplate

#Extract the details from the PDF files
def get_pdf_from_text(pdf_doc):
    text = ""
    pdf_reader = PdfReader(pdf_doc)
    for page in pdf_reader.pages:
        text += page.extract_text()
    return text
#Extract data from pdf
def extract_data_from_pdf(pages_data):

    template = """Extract the values :Patient name, Medical Conditions, Medications,
Procedures, Dates , Diagnosis , Fees from the data: {pages}
```

```python
    Expected output: {{'Patient name': 'XXXX','Medical Conditions':
'XXXX','Medications': 'XXXX','Procedures': 'XXXX','Dates': 'XXXX','Diagnosis':
'XXXX', 'Fees':'$99.99'}}
    """

    prompt_template = PromptTemplate(input_variables=["pages"],
template=template)

    llm = OpenAI(temperature=.7)
    full_response=llm(prompt_template.format(pages=pages_data))

    return full_response


# iterate over the pdf files uploaded
def create_docs(user_pdf_list):

    # define the structure for extracting data
    df = pd.DataFrame({'Patient name': pd.Series(dtype='str'),
            'Medical Conditions': pd.Series(dtype='str'),
            'Medications': pd.Series(dtype='str'),
            'Procedures': pd.Series(dtype='str'),
             'Dates': pd.Series(dtype='str'),
            'Diagnosis': pd.Series(dtype='int'),
            'Fees': pd.Series(dtype='int'),
            })

    for filename in user_pdf_list:

        print(filename)
        raw_data=get_pdf_from_text(filename)

        llm_pdf_text=extract_data_from_pdf(raw_data)

        pattern = r'{(.+)}'
        match = re.search(pattern, llm_pdf_text, re.DOTALL)

        if match:
            extracted_values = match.group(1)

            # Convert the extracted text to a dictionary
```

```python
        data_dict = eval('{' + extracted_values + '}')
        print(data_dict)
    else:
        print("No records found with matching criteria.")

    df=df._append([data_dict], ignore_index=True)
    df.head()
    return df
```

8.4.3   *PDF file name1: JamesMartin.pdf*

ABCD Clinic, Plano, TX
Phone: 679-987-2021

Date: Jan-03-2024

Patient name: James Martin

Medical Conditions: Severe head-ache for the last 3 days

Medications: Aleeve is to be administered for 3 times a day. Blood pressure is to be tested.
Exercise is recommended for 40 minutes a day.

Procedures: Take Blood pressure test and check for any sinus problems.

Dates: Please visit hospital on Jan-11-2024 for follow-ups.

Diagnosis: Normal pain detected. Expected to cure in weeks time.

Fees: $125.75

8.4.4 PDF file name2: JacquelineGeorge.pdf

ABCD Clinic, Plano, TX
Phone: 679-987-2021

Date: Jan-03-2024

Patient name: Jacquelin George

Medical Conditions: Severe fever of 102 degrees with head-ache, runny nose, cough and sneezing conditions.

Medications: Tylenol to be administered 3 times a day. Hot water is to be taken. Complete rest is needed.

Procedures: Flu test and Covid test are recommended.

Dates: *Please visit hospital on Jan-10-2024 for follow-ups.*

Diagnosis: *COVID virus is detected.*

Fees: $250.50

8.4.5 File name: .env

OPEN_API_KEY="YOUR_OPENAI_API_KEY"

8.4.6 File name: .env.sample

OPEN_API_KEY=""

Extract Clinical Documents

Extracting clinical documents

Upload the clinical documents here in PDF format

| ☁ | **Drag and drop files here**
Limit 200MB per file • PDF | **Browse files** |

| 🗋 | JacquelinGeorge.pdf 54.0KB | ✕ |
| 🗋 | JamesMartin.pdf 38.6KB | ✕ |

Extract Data

	Patient name	Medical Conditions	Med
0	James Martin	Severe head-ache for the last 3 days	Alee
1	Jacquelin George	Severe fever of 102 degrees with head-ache, runny nose, cough and sneezing conditic	Tyle

Download data as CSV

	A	B	C	D	E	F	G
1	Patient name	Medical Conditions	Medications	Procedures	Dates	Diagnosis	Fees
2	James Martin	Severe head-ache for the last 3 days	Aleeve is to be administered for 3 times a day.	Take Blood pressure test and check for any sinus problems.	Please visit hospital on Jan-11-2024 for follow-ups.	Normal pain detected. Expected to cure in weeks time.	$125.75
3	Jacquelin George	Severe fever of 102 degrees with head-ache, runny nose, cough and sneezing conditions.	Tylenol to be administered 3 times a day. Hot water is to be taken. Complete rest is needed.	Flu test and Covid test are recommended.	Jan-10-2024	COVID virus is detected.	$250.50
4							
5							

8.4.9 *Conclusion*

From the above example, we can understand that we have:

- Defined a prompt template to extract the required elements from the PDF file.
- Included the format of the output elements in the prompt.
- During extraction, the elements extracted match with those stored in a data dictionary.
- Finally, the data dictionary is converted into a data frame and returned to the user to extract as a CSV file.

This model can be used not only for clinical data analysis but also for extracting details from resumes, bank checks, insurance documents, etc.

Copyrighted Material

9. Challenges and Considerations

We should be considering that Prompt engineering must address concerns related to biases in model outputs. We need to design the prompts very carefully and ongoing evaluation is also necessary to mitigate biases and ensure fair language generation.

Interpretability: This involves using a model to perform a task by providing instructions in a suitable manner at the same time interpreting the results generated by the model for our requirements.

If we provide too complex instruction through the prompt template, the model may not be able to interpret your request and will respond with inaccurate results. On the other hand, if we provide instruction in a simple manner, we may not be able to capture all nuances of the response as expected.

Generalization: The models that are trained on a particular task may not perform well when we employ the model for a different requirement. For example, a model trained generating beautiful poems might have limitations when it's expected to perform text summarization, translation or for sentiment analysis tasks.

On the other hand, a model trained on general tasks such as text summarization, question-answering or translation, may not perform well when expected to write poems. So, we need to strike a balance between generalization and specialization still being versatile to handle new tasks that we come across on the way.

Personalized Prompting: By tailoring prompts based on individual user or group needs and incorporating past information, we can effectively increase the efficiency of the model utilization.

For example, the HR system used in the corporate world can be used based on the individual rights and privileges of the user groups. For, HR manager, the system may provide admin details such as rules, implementation strategies etc. But, for an employee, the model will provide the usage details such as how to make use of earned leave/casual leave, upcoming holidays in the current year etc.

Bias Mitigation and Ethical Prompting: In the future, we might see more attention on using prompts that are aware of biases and setting ethical rules for how to give instructions. This is important for making AI in a responsible way. Prompt engineering is a key part of NLP, helping us make the most of big models. As we keep improving prompt engineering, there are cool things and challenges ahead, shaping how we interact with AI in the future.

Copyrighted Material

10. Ethical AI Practices

Understanding the ethical side of the AI responses is really important while designing prompts as we need to try to avoid content generation which could be biased, sensitive, private or may lead to security issues.

For example, let's assume that a company is developing Chatbot to help the organization's internal process. It's important to feed the model during the design time to avoid topics such as politics, religion and the model should indicate that it has been trained to answer only certain details on organizational standards. Also, the company must ensure that the customer data is maintained safe and private and the information is shared based on need-to-know basis.

11.   So, what is next?

Now, you have reached the end of this book. During this journey, you had learnt the principles of Prompt Engineering and how to apply them to utilize LLM for better responses in your applications and implementations. After mastering the basics of Prompt Engineering, I would like to share a few strategies to elevate your experience to the next level.

Next, try reading articles on LLM and model implementations from HuggingFace and GitHub and any other sites where source codes are shared.

Follow the experts on the social media platforms such as LinkedIn, Facebook, Medium.com , Analytics Vidhya, and similar sites to understand their implementations, and try running the projects they share on your platform, either on PC or Google Colab.

The above approach will give you an idea of how to implement your own applications, share them in the public domain, and request for feedback. The feedback will help you understand your progress.

Next, try implementing a complex flow involving multiple phases to meet organizational requirements. For example, you can take up the process flow involved in Materials Management, which starts with the customer's Purchase Order (PO) requesting a list of finished products. Then, the stores raise Purchase Orders for insufficient materials to manufacture the assembly, followed by Goods Receipt Note (GRN) for inspected and accepted materials, Material Rejection Notes (MRN) for the rejected materials, Bill Of Material (BOM) to get the list of raw materials from stores to the production floor and finally Delivery Note (DN) through which the finished assembly is sent to the customers based on their Purchase Order (PO)

Alternatively, you can explore the candidate recruitment process and define phases according to your preferences for implementation or take up any other scenarios.

From our end, we will also release version 2.0 of this book, where we will discuss model architectures that can be implemented to solve customer requirements. Through this, we aim to understand real-time implementation and deployment strategies better.

So, let's reconnect through "Crafting Effective Prompts 2.0!" next.

12. References

1. Chatgpt api endpoints – Enough.
   https://enough3e.org/chatgpt-api-endpoints/

2. API used - https://huggingface.co/TheBloke/Llama-2-7B-Chat-GGML/tree/main

3. Taking the Patient Journey with NetBaseQuid Social Analytics - relationshipsndhelp.
   https://www.relationshipsndhelp.com/taking-the-patient-journey-with-netbasequid-social-analytics/

4. iOS / Sr. iOS Developers – Acespritech Solutions Pvt. Ltd..
   https://acespritech.com/jobs/ios-sr-ios-developers/

5. Roots Of Liberty | Essay Yu. https://rootsofliberty.org/essay-yu/

6. Taking the Patient Journey with NetBaseQuid Social Analytics - relationshipsndhelp.

   https://www.relationshipsndhelp.com/taking-the-patient-journey-with-netbasequid-social-analytics/

7. Pharmaceutical industry has been slow to adopt electronic commerce.
   https://abdallahbattah.com/pharmaceutical-industry-has-been-slow-to-adopt-electronic-commerce/

8. Arkansas - What you need to know before you go – Go Guides.
   https://www.hotels.com/go/usa/arkansas

9. 80 Interesting Facts About Arkansas - The Fact File.
   https://thefactfile.org/arkansas-facts/

10. iOS / Sr. iOS Developers – Acespritech Solutions Pvt. Ltd..

https://acespritech.com/jobs/ios-sr-ios-developers/

11. prompt idea for chat gpt Archives - Shopchun.
    https://www.shopchun.com/tag/prompt-idea-for-chat-gpt/

12. Leung, Brian, and Tom Chau. "A Multiple Camera Tongue Switch for a Child with Severe Spastic Quadriplegic Cerebral Palsy." Disability and Rehabilitation: Assistive Technology, 2009,
    https://doi.org/10.3109/17483100903254561.

13. Bogert, Eric, et al. "Algorithmic Appreciation in Creative Tasks." 2020.

14. Transformers, explained: Understand the model behind GPT, BERT, and T5
    https://www.youtube.com/watch?v=SZorAJ4I-sA

15. Top 10 AI Jobs by 2025 - Blockchain Council.
    https://www.blockchain-council.org/ai/ai-jobs/

16. Deep Learning models in Machine Learning (ML).
    http://schneppat.com/deep-learning-models-in-machine-learning.html

17. How to Fix Python was Not Found; run without arguments? - Developer Helps.
    https://www.developerhelps.com/how-to-fix-python-was-not-found-run-without-arguments/

18. Glossary of Weather Terms: Top 50 You Should Know | Maximum Weather Instruments.
    https://www.maximum-inc.com/maximum-weather-instruments-glossary-of-terms/

19. Text Summarization | Saturn Cloud.
    https://saturncloud.io/glossary/text-summarization/

20. Revolutionizing Travel: How ChatGPT is Shaping the Future of the Industry | By Simone Puorto.
    https://www.hospitalitynet.org/opinion/4116535.html

21. Multiview Deep Learning for Image Classification - reason.town.
    https://reason.town/multiview-deep-learning/

22. Machine Learning – BriteWire.
    https://britewire.com/machine-learning/

23. Lamb, David. "Learning about Events through Involvement and Participation."
    International Journal of Event and Festival Management, 2015,
    https://doi.org/10.1108/ijefm-12-2013-0043.

24. Glossary of Weather Terms: Top 50 You Should Know | Maximum Weather
    Instruments.
    https://www.maximum-inc.com/maximum-weather-instruments-glossary-
    of-terms/

25. What does the force of gravity between two objects depend on? - QA
    StudyFAQ.
    https://qa.studyfaq.com/question/force-gravity-two-objects-depend

26. https://library.fiveable.me/ap-physics-c-m/unit-7/overview/study-
    guide/A1M4bZ1tNwlWKQa6Q6Jz

27. Snellman, Jan. "Relaxation-type Second-order Closure Models in Astrophysical
    Hydrodynamics." 2015,
    https://core.ac.uk/download/33733390.pdf

28. Hukum Yadav, Author at Square Box - Page 4 of 8.
    https://squarebox.in/author/hukum_yadav/page/4/

29. Transparent and conductive paper from nanocellulose fibers — KAUST
    FACULTY PORTAL.
    https://faculty.kaust.edu.sa/en/publications/transparent-and-conductive-
    paper-from-nanocellulose-fibers

30. Use of Fascial Closure Needle Versus Staples for Mesh Fixati | 40682.
    https://www.iomcworld.com/abstract/use-of-fascial-closure-needle-versus-
    staples-for-mesh-fixation-in-laparoscopic-transabdominal-preperitoneal-
    hernioplasty-40682.html

31. Wang, Han, et al. "A Weakly-Supervised Named Entity Recognition Machine
    Learning Approach for Emergency Medical Services Clinical Audit."

International Journal of Environmental Research and Public Health, vol. 18, no. 15, 2021, p. 7776.

32. Master LangChain Build #16 AI Apps-OpenAI,LLAMA2,HuggingFace by Sharath Raju from Udemy.com

33. ChatGPT Vs. Davinci: Which One Is Better? - The Nature Hero. https://thenaturehero.com/chatgpt-vs-davinci/

34. Revolutionary Eco-Friendly Solution Promises to Save Our Planet - News Now World. https://newsnowworld.com/revolutionary-eco-friendly-solution-promises-to-save-our-planet/

35. What is Human Resource Outsourcing?. https://www.hirequotient.com/hr-glossary/what-is-human-resource-outsourcing

36. ChatGPT's Competitors According To ChatGPT - DotCom Magazine-Influencers And Entrepreneurs Making News. https://www.dotcommagazine.com/2023/03/chatgpts-competitors-according-to-chatgpt/

37. Awards For Physical Education & Health - Hicksville Public Schools. https://lee.hicksvillepublicschools.org/cms/One.aspx?portalId=136760&pageId=1753839

38. Thompson, John. "The Contingent Workforce: The Solution to the Paradoxes of the New Economy." Strategy & Leadership, vol. 25, no. 6, 1997, pp. 44-45.

39. IT Archives - AIDEC Digital. https://aidecdigital.com/category/it/

40. Always Retrieval Augment Your Large Language Models. https://www.deepset.ai/blog/llms-retrieval-augmentation

41. Intro to Ai's and What Ai can do - Questions - Aptos. https://forum.aptoslabs.com/t/intro-to-ais-and-what-ai-can-do/245662

42. Artificial intelligence in diagnostics – A comprehensive guide for medical professionals in India - Medical Buyer.

https://www.medicalbuyer.co.in/artificial-intelligence-in-diagnostics-a-comprehensive-guide-for-medical-professionals-in-india/

43. Soni, Tanishq, et al. "Mapping the Scientific Landscape of Internet of Things and Artificial Intelligence Using VOSViewer." 2023,

    https://doi.org/10.1109/icicat57735.2023.10263692.ai
    https://blog.synctrack.io/tag/ai/

44. . "Artificial Intelligence News Reader Application." 2023, https://core.ac.uk/download/560693739.pdf.

45. How Artificial Intelligence Is Transforming Digital Marketing | Blog | Web Development Company, Oman. https://arabic.adventz.net/blog/how-artificial-intelligence-is-transforming-digital-marketing/

46. What is Artificial Intelligence : what is AI - Sarkari Network Make A Money. https://www.sarkarinetwork.xyz/2023/09/what-is-artificial-intelligence-what-is.html

47. Artificial Intelligence Interview Question And Answers - DridhOn. https://dridhon.com/artificial-intelligence-interview-question-and-answers/

48. What is Artificial Intelligence in details - Drushya Digital India. https://drushyaindia.com/what-is-artificial-intelligence-in-details/

49. Xu, Keyuan. "Stochastic Modeling of Biological Sequence Evolution." 2005, https://core.ac.uk/download/4397458.pdf

50. Vector Dot Product (Explanation and Everything You Need to Know). https://www.storyofmathematics.com/vector-dot-product

51. Dot Product: Definition, Formula, Important Properties & Examples. https://testbook.com/maths/dot-product

52. Torch is not able to use CUDA/No CUDA GPUs are available - Drivers - Linux, Windows, MacOS - NVIDIA Developer Forums.

https://forums.developer.nvidia.com/t/torch-is-not-able-to-use-cuda-no-cuda-gpus-are-available/246480

53. Zhou, Ling. "A Historical Overview of Artificial Intelligence in China." Science Insights, 2023,
https://doi.org/10.15354/si.23.re588

54. Robotic Process Automation Vs Machine Learning.
https://syscor.ai/2023/05/26/robotic-process-automation-vs-machine-learning/

55. AI vs ML vs DL: What's the Difference?.
https://www.workwithali.com/post/ai-vs-ml-vs-dl-what-s-the-difference

56. artificial intelligence Archives - WonderStacked.
https://wonderstacked.com/tag/artificial-intelligence/

57. Federal Government AI Automation: Transforming Efficiency.
https://www.convergint.com/artificial-intelligence-automation-in-the-federal-government-sector/

58. IT Archives - AIDEC Digital.
https://aidecdigital.com/category/it/

59. The Future of Prompt Engineering: Trends to Watch Out For in 2023.
https://www.reliablegroup.com/blog/the-future-of-prompt-engineering-trends-to-watch-out-for-in-2023/science | Blog 2read ðŸ"š.
https://blog.2read.net/tags/science/

60. Happiness according to Psychology - The Brain Blog.
https://thebrain.blog/happiness-psychology/

61. Quotes On Stocks. - Zaviad.
https://zaviad.com/quote/quotes-on-stocks/

62. AI Prompt Engineering: The Future of Natural Language Processing | AskGalore Digital.
https://askgalore.com/what-is-prompt-engineering/

63. Will AI-Generated Content Replace Freelance Writers? – Love Freelancing.
https://lovefreelancing.com/will-ai-generated-content-replace-freelance-writers/

64. FAQs | Christian Schools International.
https://www.csionline.org/accreditation/faqs

65. "The Impact of Age Diversity in the Classroom".
https://www.aseniorcitizenguideforcollege.com/2023/02/the-impact-of-age-diversity-in-classroom.html

66. Prompt Engineering Guide
https://www.promptingguide.ai

www.ingramcontent.com/pod-product-compliance
Lightning Source LLC
Chambersburg PA
CBHW060141060326
40690CB00018B/3932